THE COSMIC WISDOM OF JOE BOB BRIGGS

THE C⊖SMIC

Random House 🏠 *New York*

WISDOM OF

JOE BOB BRIGGS

JOE BOB BRIGGS

All rights reserved under International and
Pan-American Copyright Conventions.
Published in the United States by Random House, Inc.,
New York, and
simultaneously in Canada by Random House of Canada
Limited, Toronto.

Library of Congress Cataloging-in-Publication Data

Briggs, Joe Bob.
The cosmic wisdom of Joe Bob Briggs/ by Joe Bob Briggs.
p.   cm.
ISBN 0-394-58890-8
I. Title.
PN4874.B668A25   1990
814'.54—dc20   90-53128
CIP

Book design by Guenet Abraham
Manufactured in the United States of America

24689753

First Edition

For Rudy Bloom

CRUDE, INSENSITIVE INTRODUCTION

The Supreme Court recently made it illegal to be a smartass. It was only a matter of time, wasn't it? For the past fifteen years the country's been tightening the screws on the unrepentant. I know. I get letters.

"Although I normally appreciate the humor of your writings . . ."

This is the way they all start.

". . . you went *over the line* with blah blah blah."

And then the reader, or the special-interest group, or the government official, or the lawyer representing the aggrieved party, will launch into the reasons that I am not Sensitive.

The goal of every modern weenie newspaper columnist in America is to be Sensitive.

The religion of the twentieth century is not God, or Truth, or Family, or Knowledge, or Art. It's Sensitivity. As in, "You may be right, but your attitude doesn't show much *Sensitivity*."

Being right used to be enough.

If you're not sufficiently Sensitive, you will be attacked, reviled, and forced to watch Alan Alda movies.

If you're not Sensitive, you'll be kicked off the team.

America doesn't need any more Sensitives. America is too full of itself.

So this book is not Sensitive.

I hope it doesn't hurt your feelings.

No I don't. There I go, *lying* again, trying to be Sensitive.

See how subtle it is?

So . . . deep breath . . .

No—to answer all the letters at once—I am *not* sorry.

—Joe Bob Briggs

CONTENTS

CONTENTS

CONTENTS

CONTENTS

PART I

THE REASONS
WE'RE DOOMED

I got a letter in the mail from Montgomery Ward's telling me I could hire a Montgomery Ward's lawyer for just $6.75 a month. Naturally, since my own personal attorney, Bubba Barclay, is serving time in the Louisiana State Penitentiary, I decided you can't be too careful, and so a couple months ago I went down to Monkey Ward's to retain counsel. Of course, Bubba Barclay only charged me five bucks a month, but you had to call Bubba at a pay phone during one of the three daily rest periods in the license-plate factory. So I figured just the regular office hours alone would be worth the extra buck seventy-five.

Anyhow, when I got down there, I had to wait for about

twenty minutes because my assigned lawyer, Melvin Blevins, was over in Home Furnishings demonstrating a back-massage Strato-Lounger. I couldn't blame him, cause the commissions on those things are outstanding, and the wait gave me time to look through the Monkey Ward "Legal Services" brochure:

"Through this Plan, you retain the services of licensed attorneys, who are in private practice in your community, for a set fee of $6.75 per month. Yes. These are the same attorneys who may charge $75 per hour and more to the general public. . . . According to the American Bar Association, you and every other law abiding citizen have a 37 per cent probability of running into a legal problem within a year. . . . Make no mistake: Life is not fair. Your legal rights are constantly being challenged, in leases, contracts, banking transactions, warranty and consumer complaints. In many cases, your satisfaction is *not* guaranteed. . . ."

And it went on and on, telling me how I was gonna get outlawyered by some corporation in the next three hours, and so by the time Melvin came over to talk to me, I blurted out, "Melvin, do I still have time? I'm afraid somebody might have sued me while you were selling that set of patio furniture."

But Melvin reassured me that I *was* protected. "Not only can we sign you up to the Montgomery Ward Legal Services Plan today and cover any problem you might have, but you look like a man who could use a Weedeater."

"Well, I know my yard's kinda trashed right now, but . . ."

"That's what I thought. If you buy a Weedeater today, we can add to the contract free negotiations with any ex-wife who might call you or threaten to sue you in the future."

"Boy, you guys do your homework!"

"That's why they call us . . . heh heh heh . . . attorneys."

Melvin had to run over and do a price check on a pair of orange thongs, and I started to think, "Hey! Wait a minute here! How do I know I'm getting the absolute top-of-the-line legal advice? What if this guy made bad grades in law school?" And so, when Melvin got back, I decided to ask him a few trick questions.

"By the way, Melvin," I said as casually as I could, "what exactly is habeas corpus?"

"Let's break it down and take a look at it," Melvin said. " 'Habeas' is the Latin word for venereal disease, from the ancient name for tiny little growths, or habeas, on the skin. And 'corpus,' of course, is a dead body. We all know that. A little child knows that. So what you have there is a guy that died of herpes. Habeas corpus. Or, more precisely, a dead body covered with disgusting growths. That's basically what you're dealing with there."

I was impressed, but I tried not to let him know. Just to make sure he knew what he was talking about, I said, "What's a brief?"

"A brief," Melvin said, "is a male undergarment, sold in several colors in the Men's Wear and Sports Wear departments."

I knew about Men's Wear, but it was the Sports Wear answer that convinced me. You might know a *little* about a subject, but it takes a lawyer to know the whole story.

I pulled out my Monkey Ward's charge card and told Melvin I was ready to spring for the six-seventy-five, but I had one more legal concern.

"You know, Melvin, most people get arrested at two in the morning when the topless bars let out. What happens if I need you after closing time?"

"No problem," Melvin told me. "You just send a friend to the

Montgomery Ward's Car Care Center, and you'll see the Early Bird message box there on the outside of the building. Take an envelope, fill it out, and where it says 'Describe repairs,' write, 'In jail, need to get out.' Be sure to specify which jail. And when the service manager comes in at six A.M., he'll deal with it right away."

"He'll come get me out of jail?"

"Depends on how many cars are in front of you, but he'll get to it just as soon as he can."

"Sounds like an okay deal to me. Preciate it, Mel."

And so I signed the deal, six-seventy-five a month, and it turned out to be the smartest money I ever spent. Just one month after I employed Melvin Blevins as my lawyer, I was doing this real estate deal that turned ugly at the last minute and so I ended up being sued by seven Fortune 500 corporations, three accounting firms, and the attorney general of the state of Texas. It's all just one big misunderstanding. The most I could get is thirty-five years in prison, a million-dollar fine, and $45 million in damages, and so you probly think I'm worried.

Naw. When they called and said, "Melvin Belli will be representing our consolidated action," I called back and said, "So what, you turkeys! My lawyer is Monkey Ward's!"

I'm sure it'll only be a matter of days now before they get scared and drop the case.

WHY LONNIE CAN'T READ AND DOESN'T GIVE A FLIP

Have yall heard how the new high schools work?

I have a nephew named Lonnie Phipps who's been living at the trailer house, trying to finish twelfth grade while his parents are off in Florida arguing over who was meaner and so doesn't deserve to get the dresser set and bureau that Grandma had. And Lonnie's been bringing his report card home all year and all it had on it was A's and one B, and so I was thinking about having Lonnie write some speeches for me, except I reconsidered when I remembered that Lonnie never talks. He mostly sits in front of the TV set and watches ESPN Australian Rules Football, that game where the object is to sling mud on your face and kick a giant ball into your opponent's head until the umpire raises up his arms and gives you some points, for no apparent reason.

Anyhow, Lonnie brought home this letter that said he got a combined 485 on his SATs. I don't know how much you know about the SATs, but that's like an F. Naw, it's not the worst you can get. It's like an F-plus.

So I got Lonnie by the scruff of the neck and slouched down to school with him, and went in and talked to Lonnie's English teacher, and I said, "Miz Stinson"—she was this tired-lookin bent-over lady with too much cheek makeup—"Miz Stinson, Lonnie here made A's in your class all year, and these SAT people, they say that basically he couldn't play *Wheel of Fortune* even if the clue was 'Animal' and it had three letters and the first one was a *d* and the third one was a *g*. He wouldn't even get the *concept* of it."

And Miz Stinson, she said, "Lonnie is reading at above-average level for the school."

(I should point out right here that Lonnie goes to one of those public schools where they bus in blacks, Mexicans, white trash, yuppies, Vietnamese, and, most horrifying of all, people who have recently relocated from California. The goal is to never meet any person in the hall who's even remotely like yourself.)

And so I said to Miz Stinson, "What is the reading level for this school?"

And she said, "We have an eighty-two percent passing rate on the TEAMS test for English."

And I said, "What the heck is the TEAMS test for English?"

And she went into this long explanation about how the Texas Legislature was concerned about too many kids getting A's and B's and still not knowing how to read or add up numbers, and so they started giving this TEAMS test in Math and English, and if you don't pass the TEAMS test, then you don't graduate. And then she talked about how most of Lonnie's training for the last year was *training to take the TEAMS test.*

"How can you teach a boy that still picks his nose how to take a test before the test comes?"

"We have outlines of the basic material that will be covered on the TEAMS test," she said.

"Lemme get this straight. You *already know* what the questions are gonna be on the TEAMS test?"

"No. We know general areas. For example, the reading comprehension portion always deals with *Animal Farm.*"

"You mean *Animal Farm* by George Orwell? The book about talkin pigs that hasn't been worth reading for about forty years now?"

"Oh, all our students read it."

"Whatever happened to *Silas Marner* and *A Midsummer Night's Dream* and *The Grapes of Wrath?* Don't you always read those in senior English? I went to school in Hooks, Texas, where most people can't even read the name stitched over their own pocket, and we *all* had to read that stuff."

"We've found that *Animal Farm* is the most manageable book for seniors."

"Because it's only twenty pages long! Any other book, they might have to learn to *read* first!"

So anyway, Miz Stinson and me went at it for a while longer, but the way it turns out is, all they do in the English class for the *entire year* is learn how to take the Texas Legislature graduation test.

"Perhaps," Miz Stinson said, using the word "perhaps" for about the fiftieth time, "perhaps Lonnie needs some special counseling in how to take a test."

"What do you mean, how to take a test?"

"We find that many of the students don't do well on the test because they are culturally unfamiliar with testing procedures."

"Lonnie knows how to color in a little box with a number-two pencil, if that's what you're talking about."

"Lonnie is a very bright student," she said. At that moment Lonnie was scrunched down in his chair like a fat man's sofa cushion, pickin burrs off his blue jeans. "I would recommend that Lonnie see the testing tutor."

"And what does the testing tutor do? Teach him how to spell his name, I hope."

"The testing tutor would be able to help Lonnie understand what he's being asked on the test."

"Listen to me, lady! He *understands* what he's being asked on the test. He does *not* understand what to *answer* on the test."

"You must understand," she said, "with the system being what it is, that we barely have time to get these students ready for this test. We can't give them a lot of individual attention."

"Lonnie doesn't need individual attention. He needs somebody standing in front of a blackboard saying, 'Lonnie, notice that there's only two *e*'s in the word 'cheek,' not *four*, the way *you* spelled it.' And lemme ask you one more question. If the only purpose of high school is to pass this Texas Legislature test, then what are the report cards for? What do all the A's and B's mean? What exactly are those letters *reporting* on the card?"

"That would indicate," she said, "that Lonnie is in the top ten percent of his class."

"That's what I was afraid of. You got anything to say, Lonnie?"

"Yeah." Lonnie tensed his forehead muscles. Sometimes Lonnie *forgets* what he wants to say.

"What is it, Lonnie?"

"I don't really care if I graduate," he said. "I know it's not the way I'm supposed to feel, but I don't care."

"Lonnie, you shouldn't say that," Miz Stinson said. "A high school diploma is something you'll need later on in life."

"Lady," I said, "you obviously don't expect there to be much going on in this boy's life."

When we got home, I told Lonnie he was right. I'd consider him a weenie if he *does* graduate. Miz Stinson needs to go back and read *Animal Farm* thirty, forty more times, till she figures out the parts that deal specifically with her.

POL POT'S LOVE CONNECTION

You ever get hooked on this show called *The Love Connection*, where people go on a blind date and then go on TV and make fun of each other's hairdos while Chuck Woolery screws up his face and says stuff like, "Leon! What do you mean you don't like to date girls who have clefts in their chins?"? And then the audience boos and hisses because Leon just went on a date with a girl with a cleft chin. And then the girl says, "Chuck, you wouldn't believe the kind of car he was driving, and he hadn't cleaned it in a month!" And then Leon says, "Why should I clean it, just so you can put your 340-pound rear end on my upholstery?" And now the audience is cheering for *Leon*, because the girl shouldn't have told him his car was dirty.

You ever been hooked on this show? I think it's an amazing show. But here's the most amazing thing about it:

The people that go on these dates always know *immediately*, as soon as the guy comes over to pick the gal up, as soon as they *open the door*—they know whether this is gonna be a good date or a bad date. Because the first question Chuck always asks is, "So what did you think of him when you saw him?"

What would be a normal answer to that question? Wouldn't it be something like, "Well, Chuck, I'd only known the guy for five seconds, how could I have an opinion about him? That would be pretty shallow of me to form any conclusions about the guy based on how he knocked on my door, and what expression he had on his face when I opened it."

But, of course, this has never, ever been the answer they give.

"Well, Chuck, he really wasn't what I'd expected from talking to him on the phone. He told me he looked like Richard Gere, but he looked more like Richard Gere's mother. He had on a Hawaiian shirt, Chuck! He was wearing a Hawaiian shirt for our date!"

And then they ask the guy the same question.

"She was a very attractive woman, but she had an attitude, Chuck. She wouldn't look at me. She had a neighbor come over to her house before I got there. I felt like they were sizing me up together. I thought that was kinda rude, Chuck."

This is about 90 percent of the dates on the show. Then, in about 10 percent of the cases, the answer will be:

"She was a classy woman, Chuck. Very impressive."

Nothing about what she did. Nothing about what she said. Nothing about what she was wearing. In other words, they only start talking about the details if they *don't* like the person. If they *like* the person, then they say:

"Chuck, he was so cute. He had on a Hawaiian shirt. It was just like something Richard Gere would do."

What they should do, to make this show more realistic, is not go on the date at all. Just bring some people onstage, put the guys on one side of a door, the gals on the other, and then, couple by couple, *open* the door. "What do you think?" Chuck would say.

"Well, Chuck, I know that if we went on a date, she would pig out on lobster and then criticize every place I wanted to take her."

"Chuck, he's not my type. I like men with chins. Chins are very important to me."

And then about one in a hundred would say, "Mighty fine, Chuck."

And she would say, "He's like a dream come true, Chuck."

And then they could get married right there on the show.

Do you understand what I'm saying here? People aren't interested in finding a person they can fall in love with. They're interested in finding a person they've *already* fallen in love with. He's rooting around there in their brain, and all they have to do is find some person who *looks* like him.

Or there's another way we could do. It's called the Pol Pot Love Connection Game.

When Pol Pot was the dictator in Cambodia, he had these concentration camps where he would chain a man and a woman together so they would be forced to have sex and he could build up the population. The man and the woman were picked at random, and they would be chained together for up to two years, living in these work camps full of disease and poverty and hunger. And then Pol Pot was finally defeated, and the prisoners who were still living were freed of their chains.

And now, ten years later, many of those couples who were

chained together are deciding to get married. To *each other*! They're having big formal weddings.

Now how can this be?

They didn't like each other any more than the *Love Connection* people do when they first saw each other.

So what's the difference between the Chuck Woolery way and the Pol Pot way?

The Pol Pot way forced them to get to know the *whole person*. They were chained to him when he was sick, when he was angry, when he was weak, when he was helpful, when he was clean, when he was dirty, when he was in fear for his life. And, eventually, a lot of stuff didn't matter anymore. It didn't matter, for example, what he was wearing when they met and what he said at the time. It didn't matter what the gal expected him to be. These Cambodian lovers ended up falling in love with a real person, a person who never existed in their own heads.

I'm not saying we should chain up these *Love Connection* people and stick em in a concentration camp to show em what love is, because you know what they'd say?

"Chuck, you wouldn't believe it. He was wearing a *chain* around his neck. He expected me to be interested in *that*. And he had these icky whip burns on his back."

"She wasn't even wearing makeup, Chuck."

And Chuck could say, "Well, it was probably difficult to find makeup there in the concentration camp."

"It just wasn't what I was looking for, Chuck."

"He had no shirt on, Chuck."

"I'm not looking for a forced imprisonment in my life. I'm not ready for that right now."

Now that I think about it, maybe I *am* saying we should stick these people in a concentration camp.

I've been studying Junk Bonds. I'm trying to understand. I think I understand. If you understand what Junk Bonds are, and you wanna help me, then write me a letter. But, as of today, when they're fresh on my mind, I'm gonna put down what I *think* they are.

You've probly heard people talking about Junk Bonds, usually when some huge mother of a megahumongous corporation goes out of business.

"How could the hundred-year-old American Refrigerated Pork Bellies go bankrupt, just like that?"

"Junk Bonds. They had too many Junk Bonds."

Or: "What happened to the stock-brokerage firm of Wheasel, Gouge, and Lye? They were *famous!*"

"Junk Bonds. They sold too many Junk Bonds. In fact, Wheasel, Gouge was the firm that invented the Junk Bonds sold by American Refrigerated Pork Bellies."

And so, after a while, you hear these stories about Junk Bonds, and you're thinking, "Didn't anybody ever think that maybe just the *name* was a dead giveaway?"

"Hey, wanna buy a couple these Junk Bonds? Maybe we can get rich enough off these things to buy a few junk cars, maybe some junk dinette sets, or a little junk jewelry. Then, if we get *really* rich, we can become junk dealers. We might even become *junkies.*"

How does something like this happen? How do people spend ten years buying and selling something with "junk" in the name, and then say, "Oh my God, you mean those weren't good investments? They sounded so *great*! Junk Bonds. We thought we couldn't go wrong with a name like that."

Who are these people?

And so this led me to ask the question, "Just what *is* a Junk Bond anyhow?"

And here, as near as I can figure out, is the answer.

You got some company. Let's call it Elroy Marples Aluminum Siding of Slidell, Louisiana. Elroy is making good money. He's got loyal customers. But he's not growing fast enough to suit him. So he decides he's gonna expand into Bogalusa. But Bogalusa's already got Boone Swisher Aluminum Siding and Satellite Dishes Corporation, and it's a whole lot bigger than Elroy's company. But Boone Swisher's getting on up there in years, and he might be ready to retire. So Elroy decides to make him a cash offer for his company.

Only one problem: Elroy doesn't have that much money. Boone's company is three times bigger than Elroy's, so he can't borrow that much money, either. I guess that leaves Elroy out in the cold, doesn't it? I guess he'll just have to do everything the old-fashioned way, like opening a little office in Bogalusa and going into competition with Boone and building his new company from the ground up.

But *no*! There *is* an answer for Elroy!

It's called an Investment Banker!

The Investment Banker shows up—let's call him Banker Bob—and he says, "I can get you all the cash you *need* to buy Boone Swisher's company."

And Elroy says, "I ain't got the capital."

And Banker Bob says, "Don't need no capital."

And Elroy says, "I can't get the loan."

And Banker Bob says, "Don't need no loan."

And Elroy says, "What do I need then?"

And the Investment Banker says, "We'll write you up a Junk Bond."

And Elroy says, "What's a Junk Bond?"

And Banker Bob says, "It's real simple. We sell these pieces of paper to people all over America—pension funds, PTAs, unions. And whatever they pay us, you use that money to buy Boone Swisher Aluminum Siding and Satellite Dish Corporation."

"And what's it say on those papers?" Elroy asks him.

And Banker Bob says, "It just says you'll pay the people back."

And so Elroy says, "Why would they wanna give me this money any more than the bank would?"

"Because you're gonna pay them a whole heck of a lot more interest than you'd be paying the bank. The bank would only want ten percent. You're gonna pay these people about seventeen percent—you know, like when you get behind on your Visa."

"Oh yeah? And they'd do that?"

"Easy as pie. Junk Bonds. Everbody wants one."

"And I guess I'd pay that money back from . . ."

"Well, see here, that's the beauty of it," says Banker Bob. "You're gonna *immediately* sell off the Satellite Dish part of Boone Swisher Aluminum Siding and Satellite Dish Corporation. And so you'll get a big hunk of change for that. Cause the only part you really want is the aluminum-siding part. And then, see, you'll not only have all your usual Slidell business, but you'll also have Bogalusa business, and so that's double the income, plus you can jack up the price ten, twenty percent just by having a monopoly in the Greater Slidell–Bogalusa area."

"Makes sense to me," says Elroy. "What do you call this again?"

"We call em Junk Bonds."

"Where'd you get that name, anyhow?"

"Well, you couldn't get a loan from anywhere else besides me. That right there makes em Junk Bonds."

"Oh."

And so Elroy gets real excited, and he buys out Boone Swisher, and he consolidates all the aluminum-siding business on the Pearl River, and then one day he starts making those interest payments on the Junk Bonds, and he says "Whoa! This is one of them loan-shark deals, isn't it?" Cause he sees he's gonna have to be ponying up $38,000 every month, and he's only got about $54,000 coming in, and he's got employees, and he's got a trailer-house office, and he's got phone lines—and so then he remembers: time to sell off the Satellite Dish part of the business, to raise cash.

Surprise! Nobody wants to *buy* a satellite-dish business. Everbody's already bought their satellite dishes. There's one old boy over in Picayune, Mississippi, who comes by to look at the dishes one day, says he'll take em for scrap, but other than that, there's no market for satellite-dish retailers. But Elroy needs the cash real bad, and times get tighter and tighter, and so finally he sells off the old dishes to the boy in Picayune to make a few late Junk Bond payments.

But he's still got those $38,000 payments due ever month, like clockwork, and one thing he forgot to consider is that, being such a big company now, trying to serve all the aluminum-siding needs of Slidell and Bogalusa, he's burning gas all up and down Highway 41, he's calling long distance fifty times a day, he's got overhead out the wazoo.

And so finally old Elroy keels over dead one day from the stress, and his widow goes and looks at the ruins of Elroy Marples Aluminum Siding, and the lawyer tells her, "Well, ain't nothing to do but put it in Chapter Seven bankruptcy."

And the Widow Marples says, "How in heck did this happen?"

And the lawyer says, "Had something to do with Junk Bonds."

"Somebody slipped him some fake bonds?"

"No, it was a *good* thing, these Junk Bonds."

"Right," she says. "I can tell by the name."

"Too bad about all those teachers' pension funds that bought the Junk Bonds, though. They'll lose all their money."

"That's such a shame. How could they have ever known? Whoever was running their pension fund went to em and said, 'Hey, you guys, we've got guaranteed security *forever* now! We're buying *Junk Bonds!*' I mean, who *wouldn't* think that was the right thing to do?"

"Never could have been predicted."

"Nope. Junk Bonds. Sounds like gold to me."

Isn't this about what happened? Correct me if I'm wrong, but isn't this why people are jumping out of windows in New York City?

THE SLEAZE METER

All the newspapers in Bogotá, Colombia, had big headlines and editorials about the Dee Cee mayor getting arrested for being a coke-head. They were even gloating about it. "You can't pin *this* one on us," they were saying. "The number-one guy in the capital of America was buying Colombian farm products. Try to tell us *this* guy is a victim."

But the fact is, there were people in Dee Cee who *were* saying Mayor Barry was a victim. They showed up outside the courthouse with signs, claiming the guy was set up by the FBI for political reasons. (I'm not blaming the mayor for thinking people were out to get him. When you use coke, you think *everybody* is out to get you.)

Anyhow, the interesting thing to me is that, during the first couple of days after the guy was arrested, people weren't talking so much about how pitiful it was. They were wondering *if* this would affect the guy's political career. Like, "Sure he does a lot of coke, but he doesn't snort during the actual city council meetings. *Give the man a break!*"

Even the press was being nice to him for a while. And then reality set in after three, four days, and the reporters thought, "Wait a minute. What am I? What is my purpose in life? Oh yeah, that's right. I'm supposed to *bury* this guy." It's the John "Womanizing" Tower Principle. Occasionally even a coyote gets so full that it couldn't eat another sheep even if you butchered it and left it on a rock. The coyote has to wait two, three days until it's hungry again. I think that's basically what was happening here with Marion Barry.

But, in the meantime, this strange mercy on the part of the press—those two days when they were asking the question, "Well, I don't know, do you think he *could* snort coke and still be the mayor?"—made me realize just how high the Sleaze Meter rating has gone the past couple of years for politicians. We don't ask how sleazy they are anymore. We *know* they're sleazy. Otherwise, they wouldn't be in office. We just ask, "Is the guy too sleazy to remain in office, or is he *just sleazy enough* to be a public servant?"

And I think we've found the *exact point* on the Sleaze Meter where we're *not quite sure.* Everybody on the high side of "Coke User" gets drummed out of office. But anybody below that gets the benefit of the doubt.

The Meter runs like this:

1. Total disregard for the public: About a 10 on the meter. This is not even considered sleazy anymore. It's considered being "independent."

2. Taking political contributions from sleazeball government contractors: 20 on the Sleaze Meter. No big deal. You have to get nailed on some totally unrelated charge before a reporter is gonna plow through your campaign records.

3. Heavy drinker: 30 on the Sleaze Meter. This used to be a requirement for holding public office, but now the press considers it interesting copy. Nothing you could ever lose your job over. In fact, if you check into Betty Ford, the Sleaze Meter goes back to zero.

4. Sleeping with your secretary: 40 on the Sleaze Meter. Can go as high as 60 on the Sleaze Meter if the story is written by a female reporter, or by a male reporter who is sleeping with his secretary.

5. Sexual harassment of your secretary, your summer interns, or your page: 50 on the Sleaze Meter. Enough to get a *nasty* little article in the *Post*. The harassment can't get you into trouble, but cute little coeds from Duke University can file actual *lawsuits* these days. This can go as high as 80 on the Sleaze Meter if the article is written by a female reporter who has never been sexually harassed in her life.

6. Actual bribes: A 60 on the Sleaze Meter and a felony, but you probly won't get caught. Most bribes are business bribes, and business bribes are boring copy. The only politician who made bribery into a form of High Sleaze was the Tennessee governor indicted for selling pardons to convicted murderers. The Sleaze Meter doesn't apply to people who are actually brain-damaged.

7. Frequenting prostitutes: A 70 on the Sleaze Meter, but only because the hookers have started writing books. Any-

one can survive a trip to a brothel, but nobody can survive the Random House publicity campaign.

8. Coke user: A good solid 80. We used to send 80s to the political slaughterhouse, but Mayor Barry is breaking new ground in sleaze here. This is the crucial crossover point.

9. Murder: A 90 on the Sleaze Meter. A political career can theoretically survive one murder, if it's provoked, if you kill a very unpopular person, and if you weren't cheating on that person at the time. But it's not advised.

10. Mass murder: A perfect 100. Taking an AK-47 into the Senate chamber to vent your rage probly wouldn't pass muster with the Washington press corps. We'll have to wait another five, six years for that.

OUR BRAINS ARE

ALREADY FRIED

They just found out that your Mr. Coffee machine might be emitting killer death rays. It's something about the "electromagnetic fields," which is one of those ideas that makes my eyes glaze over because it reminds me of all the D's I made in science. But the bottom line is: Electric blankets can kill.

Anything with a wire coming out of it can zap your cells and make your ectoplasm quiver and your ribosomes go to Vegas. If you're around super-industrial-strength appliances, like video screens, then all the death waves can kung-fu your mitochondria and make your chromosomes speak in tongues. This accounts, of course, for the recent spate of three-headed babies demanding brand-new Nikes in Palo Alto, California.

At first I didn't believe this stuff. I mean, come on, you're gonna use your toaster *one* too many times and—whap!—you get giant green fungus in your armpit. But in fact, this is exactly what's been happening. Just a few examples from public health files:

1. In Oshkosh, Wisconsin, a housewife named Marian Strindberg was using an upright vacuum cleaner when, after about an hour of intensive cleaning, she suddenly sucked her three-year-old son, Chad, into the dust-collection bag and attempted to deposit the bagged child in an outdoor Hefty trash container. Neighbors, alerted by the sound of Chad coughing up carpet bunnies, intervened and saved the boy's life. Marian was found inside the house, writing a letter to the manufacturer, requesting a larger dust-collection bag attachment. A scientific team from the University of Wisconsin studied the vacuum cleaner for two weeks and determined it was emitting tiny micromagnetic waves that were broadcasting the message "You don't have to take this bull" into Marian's subconscious cell structure. Obviously, the product had to be taken off the market.

2. Julian McKendree, a gay postal carrier in Winchester, Tennessee, purchased an erotic neon sculpture called "Rigid #1." But when the sculpture was switched on, its pulsating purple neon bulb emitted infrared rays that caused Julian to dine twelve nights in a row at Steak and Ale, where he refused to order anything except sour-cream baked potatoes with chives. Julian was removed from government service and now runs a Malaysian tea-importing

business in Gatlinburg, Tennessee, where he has recurring nightmares about breadsticks.

3. Sol Steinmetz of Studio City, California, a sitcom writer best known for his hit series *Hey, You Guys!*, worked under the same fluorescent lamp for six nights in a row and immediately started writing lines like "Hi, honey, I'm home!" and "Looks like we've got company" and "Hon, I think we should talk." He has never recovered, and now languishes in syndication.

4. Steven C. Braden, a bond trader at Stephenson Zenith & McGillicuddy on Wall Street, suddenly started frothing at the mouth one morning, purchased $5 billion worth of Cleveland Municipal Water Bonds, and then announced to the firm he wanted to move to Cleveland so he could "watch my investment." Braden was subsequently diagnosed as having a brain tumor caused by constant use of a small TV set that broadcasts the Financial News Network. Efforts were made to remove the tumor, but the surgery was blocked by a Stephenson Zenith & McGillicuddy lawsuit, claiming that the tumor had actually made Braden a better bond trader. The Cleveland water bonds were sold a week later at a profit of $750,000. Braden is now required to report for work at 4:00 A.M. so he can spend at least two hours with his head resting on the screen of a thirty-nine-inch Panasonic.

5. Ronald Reagan has used an electric razor every day of his life.

6. Secret files, recently obtained through the Freedom of Information Act, reveal that in 1943 the Russians gave birth to the first test-tube baby, smuggled it into the United States, and exposed it to varying levels of microwaves from

hair dryers, irons, blenders, and—at least three times a day—washed the baby in an electric dishwasher. This cruel and inhuman experiment didn't bear fruit until more than forty years later, when the young test-tube baby landed a highly visible position in the American media. That baby was Geraldo Rivera.

I rest my case.

I LOVE YOU, AND OTHER LIES

There's this great article in *Newsweek* about how males and females talk to each other when they hate each other's guts. Like Bob calls home from the office and says, "This new secretary we hired last week is one of the nicest people I ever worked with." And then Liz answers, "That's nice." See, what Liz is *really* saying is, "The slutty little bimbo has her breasts hanging in your face all day or else you'd never even notice the tramp."

This is nonverbal communication. And it's our job as sensitive, feeling human beings to know *exactly* what people mean when they make *loaded* comments like "That's nice." And then, if we do that, we'll stop getting divorced every six months.

Fortunately, I'm an expert at human communication. I always know exactly what Wanda Bodine means when she says, "Joe Bob, did Deke Simpson pay you yesterday or do you have to wait till Friday?" That particular sentence would be translated as follows: "Joe Bob, I was just watching TV and a commercial for the Abdominizer came on and I don't have the $19.95 to send in and so I thought I would mooch it off you."

If you haven't figured this stuff out yet, then you need to, for the sake of your relationship. Here, try this example, and see if you can guess what the person is *really* saying before you read it.

LUANNE: "I picked your underwear up off the floor again." (Real meaning: "You've got the personality of a rhesus monkey, and I plan to change my hair color tomorrow, go out to a singles bar, and find somebody better.")

DEXTER: "Thank you, hon. I was so tired last night I just forgot." (Real meaning: "Elephant Hips is on the rag again.")

LUANNE: "Did you remember to get the concert tickets?" (Meaning: "I know you didn't get the concert tickets, and I know you *don't care* you didn't get the concert tickets, so I thought I'd try to make you feel like the irresponsible slope-headed piece of discount furniture that you are.")

DEXTER: "I was planning to go on my lunch hour today." (Meaning: "You know I'm lying but you *can't prove it*, and if you try to, you're a bigger bitch than I thought.")

LUANNE: "Have a good day at the office." (Meaning: "Fall in front of a bakery truck and get your head crushed under the rear tire.")

DEXTER: "Love you, honey." (Meaning: "Please, God, get me out of this.")

Okay, now try this nonverbal exercise between two strangers who are just "feeling each other out" for the first time.

JULIAN: "You are *definitely* the hottest girl on the dance floor." (Meaning: "Do you think maybe you would take off all your clothes later?")

BETSY: "Thank you." (Meaning: "Why do dorks with patches on their elbows always want to talk to *me*?")

JULIAN: "You come here a lot?" ("If I get you to talk first, then I can pretend to be whatever you want me to be and maybe you will take your clothes off later.")

BETSY: "This is the first time." ("Don't you understand body language, you dufus? Don't you realize my arms are crossed, my legs are crossed, and I'm facing away from you? What do you need, a billboard?")

JULIAN: "I normally don't come to places like this, either. It's not really a very good way to meet people." ("How long do we have to talk like this before you like me? That was a pretty cool thing to say, so I think you should be my girlfriend now.")

BETSY: ("Maybe if you didn't have giant nose hairs, someone could stand to look at you for more than two seconds at a time.") "No, I guess not."

JULIAN: ("Oh, my God, I don't know what else to say, I'm in silence, seconds are ticking by, there's a huge gulf between us and it's widening, whatever I say right here has got to be incredibly cool or I'll never get to see what she looks like naked, this is your chance, don't blow it.") "Did you drive here in a car?"

BETSY: ("No, I rented a bobsled. I don't know if I can control myself. I'm about to burst out laughing, and if I do, it'll be too embarrassing.") "Do you know where the ladies' room is?"

JULIAN: ("What if she doesn't come back?") "It's right over there."

BETSY: "Thank you." ("Hallelujah! Yippee! Hooooooooooo-ooray!")

JULIAN: "See you later." ("Maybe she didn't notice the car remark. I'll just wait right here. She'll be back in a minute.")

I suggest you keep these examples on a card in your wallet, so you're never caught without emotional translation assistance.

N ow that the Fetus Fans have won their court battle, I'd like to suggest some measures we can take to make the next eighteen years sufferable. You don't have to worry about any time *after* the next eighteen years, because by then entire armies of feti will be swarming across the country, and they'll be able to *vote*. Of course, many of em won't make it. By that time the death penalty will apply to six-year-olds and up, and many of these orphaned feti will be killing one another, in a kind of retroactive birth control.

Anyhow, here's what I think we should do. From now on each fetus should be registered. In the past all you had to do was say, "I don't want no fetus in my bod." What we should have women do now is go down to the post office as soon as they get pregnant, get a computer number for the fetus they don't want, and then go over to the courthouse steps, like you once did when you went there to say, "I will no longer be responsible for my wife's debts." Only this time you say, "Come get this here fetus."

No takers?

The county agent searches the crowd for a moment, looking for volunteer parents.

The next day somebody gets a call:

"Mr. Randolph C. Bisselman? Glad I caught you. We have a homeless fetus here and we've run a random computer matchup from a list of Pro Life activists. Congratulations! We'll be sending over Fetus No. 4789542. You might want to write that number down for your records. And I'm sure that your political, social, and religious views will shape this young fetus into a fine human being. By the way, if you'd like to view the fetus, we'd be happy to order a sonogram as soon as we locate the mother. She works, you know."

Wouldn't this work? Why not? I am *not* being facetious. Let's look at all the possible objections.

1. "That child is not my responsibility."

It's not this lady's responsibility either. She wanted sex, not a baby. In fact, this lady can't even *pronounce* "responsibility." If she gives birth to the baby, she'll probly only change its diapers once a week. This lady is the kind of lady who should have children taken *away* from her. Surely you don't want *her* to do the job?

2. "Okay, it's the government's responsibility."

You think the government is gonna take this fetus to McDonald's or buy it a GI Joe with a kung-fu grip? We got to have a human being here.

3. "Okay, a social worker should do it."

Most of em are gone—spending cuts. I've got a sister in Little Rock who runs a privately supported foster home. She's full all the time, tending all the little yard monsters she can handle. And so is just about every other foster home. Nope. We got to have some individual human beings.

4. "I don't have the money."

You've got more money than the mommy.

5. "I have my own kids to take care of."

Kids adjust to *anything*. It's *your* attitude we've got to work on.

6. "It's not fair."

Now you're talking.

7. "A baby is a full-time job, and I'm not ready for that commitment in my life right now."

Excellent.

8. "At the very least I should get some money from the government for the time I'll spend raising that baby."

Point well taken.

9. *"Nobody can do this to me!"*

Very good. Very very good. You've finally reached the emotional point of view of a poor single woman who just found out she's pregnant.

Don't worry, though, we'll all pitch in, help you out, buy the fetus a baseball bat. You just *think* you don't want it. Later it'll become the most precious thing in the world to you, because of what the two of you went through together. Trust me.

DESIGNER GENES

The National Institutes of Health got a big check from the government to study the 100 trillion cells in the human body and find out how they can mess with fetuses to upgrade the population. In other words, if I understand this deal right, they're gonna figure out exactly what each gene does and why your body is put together with little twisted ladders that have nose hairs growing out the sides. (I made D's in biology, I'm doing the best I can.)

Anyhow, there are some things about your genetic DNA that I think you ought to know, things they've already found out:

    1. They have isolated the SAT gene. When enlarged a billion times under the electron microscope, the SAT gene

shows an exact score: "567 verbal, 685 math." This means that, when the baby is born, he's already *coded* for the SAT and doesn't really need to study for it. He can if he *wants* to, but there's not really any point. You've either got a Harvard baby or a Chico State baby, and there's *nothing* you can do about it.

2. The strongest, most weather-resistant genes belong to cement contractors in the Ozark Mountains. If left unchecked, these genes will gradually dominate over all other genes in America, and we will become a race of mashed-potato-eating hawkers of concrete.

3. Researchers have discovered a "wild card" gene in independent insurance agents that causes them to put satellite dishes in their front yards.

4. We now know that Brigitte Nielsen can't help it.

5. The desire to surf is caused by a chromosomal disorder called "Dude syndrome," where the normal shapes of the 43rd and 44th chromosomes become juxtaposed in a "goofy-foot" pattern. This can be corrected with long-term therapy, but early tests show that patients lose the desire to surf but develop an even stronger desire to hang-glide.

6. *Playboy* Playmates and *Sports Illustrated* swimsuit models were tested separately for signs of any special "jiggle" genes, and it turned out that the Playmates were missing large portions of their cerebellum. This has nothing to do with genes. It was, however, a great relief to the anguished husbands of *Playboy* Playmates.

7. Fourteen-year-old boys at the East Windham Preparatory School in Bridgeport, Connecticut, were put to sleep to see if this would have any effect on their parents. Later, researchers went to the Bedford School in Asheville, North

Carolina, and reversed the process, to see if the death of a parent would have any effect on the student. In both cases, it took an average of two years for the family member to notice someone "missing." Further research showed this to be the result of what is now called the "scotch-and-soda" gene group, which also causes these people to order personalized checks with swans on them.

8. Bryant Gumbel has no genes. Researchers are looking into the possible reasons.

9. A strong faction within the federal government wants to take the genes of Marlo Thomas, graft them to the genes of Charles Manson, and see what happens. "You get that extra little oomph in the mix when you mix apples and oranges," explained one researcher. To test this idea, lab technicians are using Marlo Thomas rats—rodents that display Marlo Thomas–type behavior—and Charles Manson rats. So far the tests are inconclusive, since all the Marlo Thomas rats have devoured the Charles Manson rats.

10. A special top-secret unit of the NIH is looking into the ethical problems surrounding the search for perfect genes. Would it be ethical, for example, to eliminate a cancer gene from the population, if it also meant losing professional women's volleyball? The answer, at this point, is a probable no. "It's too much like playing God," one of the guys said. "If the Almighty put professional women's volleyball on the earth, He must have had a reason. Who are we to judge?" Another question being looked into is: "If you took all the genes from a bodybuilder like Arnold Schwarzenegger, and you injected them into the body of Pee-Wee Herman, what would it look like?" This project

has been temporarily delayed due to an outbreak of nausea among the research team doing the work.

My personal opinion of this project is that I don't think it should be left in the hands of the people with defective genes who are in charge right now. We should wait until we have much healthier genes, like maybe after we've grafted some E.T. genes onto the human race, and *then* turn these guys loose with a test tube. Otherwise one of em's gonna look up and say, "We seem to have had a little *accident* here in the lab," and then a hundred years from now we'll all have walrus teeth and hickeys on the end of our noses. Sandy Duncan would be president. It's not something you really wanna think about.

YOU'RE VERY ATTRACTIVE, BUT I'LL HAVE A PERRIER

A while back Rob Lowe checked into a sex-addiction clinic in Arizona. For about a year now I've been hearing about these places. I've even met people who told me they were in Sexaholics Anonymous. Every time they want sex, they call up a friend so they can be *talked out of it.*

I wonder what the phone calls are like?

"Herb, I need help bad. I just met this broad, and she's got bazoomas out to *here.*"

"Calm down. No, she doesn't. They're fake. You do *not* need sex with this person. What you need is . . . er . . . uh . . . what you need is . . . a bagel. Have a bagel."

And I wonder what these therapy sessions are like?

"When I married Herb, I had no idea I was marrying a *sex-aholic*! For the first three weeks he wouldn't let me out of the bedroom. One day we had sex 917 times. I mean, I have nothing against sex, but it shouldn't control your life. I felt like my entire wardrobe was being wasted."

Or what about people who marry *Playboy* Playmates?

"I guess I didn't think about it before I married her. I thought the name 'Playmate' was just an advertising gimmick. She demanded sex every time I turned around. She was a sex machine. She craved it. She lusted after me everywhere I went. Obviously, she was sick and diseased."

Now here's the interesting thing to me about these sex-addiction stories. In the sixties and seventies, you could have told these same stories, and they would have been considered *healthy*. "He has sex twelve thousand times a day. What a healthy guy." But in the nineties, all of a sudden, this makes you a sex fiend.

The scary thing is that there are doctors in charge of these clinics, which means there's a guy there who's gonna tell you exactly what "normal sex" is.

"Hey, Doc, how about five times a day?"

"No, sorry, too many."

"Three?"

"You're an addict. You need to control yourself."

"What if we just messed around on Saturday nights?"

"Now you're talking. That's what people did for *centuries*."

Then there's the guy who goes into the clinic because he messes around on his wife.

"You're sick. You should be having sex with your wife, but instead you're having it with What's-her-name."

"Tiffany."

"You're having sex with Tiffany instead of your wife."

"My wife weighs four hundred pounds. I didn't count on this when I married her."

"If you saw your wife as she *truly* is, the weight wouldn't bother you."

Actually, the guy's problem is that he *does* see his wife as she truly is, and she weighs four hundred pounds. He needs to see her as Tiffany.

"I know, Doc—I'll imagine that Tiffany weighs *five* hundred pounds."

"That's a start. At least you seem to be interested in recovery now."

Do you realize how many cartoon characters are sex addicts? Every Warner Brothers cartoon has a whistling wolf who starts jumping around on his haunches every time he sees a woman in high heels and lipstick. Obviously, this scars our children for life, turns them into froth-mouthed sexaholics.

There's a much easier way to lick this sex-addiction problem. Every time you *think* you want to have sex, just ask yourself the following questions:

    1. If I waited an hour, would I *still* want to have sex?

    2. Wouldn't something else satisfy me just as much? How about a chocolate milk?

    3. How many times have I had sex in the last three days?

    4. Is this the person I want to have sex with?

    5. If this is not the person I want to have sex with, could I find somebody else in the next hour?

    6. This person that I'm about to have sex with—the one with the cute dimples—will those dimples still be cute five minutes *after* we have sex?

    7. Do I have a heart condition?

8. Am I Catholic?

9. What if my Mom was here watching me have sex? What would she say?

10. Am I getting paid for this?

Any of these questions could result in disturbing answers that would result in either a) no sex, b) delayed sex, or c) sex with incredible guilt feelings that will keep you from having sex too much in the future.

Wouldn't this make us all much happier?

Excuse me, but with all this talk about sex, I've got to go somewhere and wait an hour.

BOVINE LAWYERS

Americans spend more money on lawyers than any nation in the world. Here's why:

A man decides to buy a Hereford cow. He sees an ad in the paper for a $600 heifer. He calls the number in the ad, inquires about the cow, drives over to look at the cow, and tells the owner of the cow, Lester Wills, "I'll take it."

Lester says, "I'll send you the papers in the mail."

Lester has spoken the magic word: "papers." There are "papers" involved. This means there are lawyers involved.

A few days later, the "papers" arrive. There is a bill of sale, a statement that the cow has no infectious diseases, a certificate showing the cow's pedigree, and a contract stating that the buyer is not allowed to resell the Hereford cow within thirty days. This seems strange, so the buyer calls Lester back.

"Lester, what is this deal about not being able to resell the cow? Not that I *want* to resell the cow. But what are you driving at here?"

"I can't remember," Lester says. "That's something the lawyer put in there. Lemme check with him."

Lester calls his lawyer. "That's standard in the industry," the lawyer says.

Whenever a lawyer can't remember why something's in a contract, he says, "That's standard in the industry."

"You need that in there," the lawyer says, "because it protects you against a rapidly changing cattle market. Let's say you had speculators in the market, and they were able to act on inside cattle information and move so fast that, before they bought the cow from you, they *already* had *another* buyer who was offering fifty bucks more. You see what's going on here? They've cheated you out of the fair market price, and there's nothing you can do about it. So the thirty-day no-resell clause protects you from being ripped off by speculators."

Lester doesn't quite understand, so he says, "Will you call this guy who's buying my cow and explain that to him?"

"Be happy to," says Lester's lawyer.

Lester's lawyer, racking up a hunnerd-buck-an-hour fee, is always "happy to."

Meanwhile, the guy buying the cow has had time to think about this no-resell clause, and he's getting mad about it. "If I buy the goldang cow," he's thinking to himself, "then I can *sell* the goldang cow, whenever I goldang please."

Then the call from the lawyer comes in. The lawyer says, "I

was asked by Lester to help you understand the no-resell clause. . . . It's really quite simple."

And now the guy *knows* he's being ripped off. So he says, "I'm sorry, but I can't discuss it with you. I'll have to consult my attorney first."

So then the would-be Hereford-buyer calls his own lawyer, and his own lawyer says, "What! They put *what* in the contract! I've never *heard* of that before! That's outrageous!"

And so now the guy is really hopping mad, and he says, "Well, I need you to call up Lester's slick lawyer and tell him that."

"I wouldn't advise you to do that," says Lawyer Number Two. "We should send him a registered letter first, so that our position will be on the record. I don't wanna end up in court on this deal."

"And what would the registered letter say?"

"It would say that the thirty-day no-resale terms are invalid, because they were not stated at the time of the deal. They weren't, were they?"

"I don't remember. I was just buying a cow. I wasn't thinking about reselling the cow."

"Where is the cow now?"

"Out in my pasture, last time I looked."

"Then the law is on our side. Possession is nine tenths of the law, you know. There's no way they can take that cow away from you."

"Lester doesn't want the cow anyhow."

"Well, send me every piece of paper that Lester's lawyer sent to you. I'll go over them and draft a response."

"Okay."

Three days later Lawyer Number Two finally calls back.

"I have the letter ready for your signature. I've added a few things that came up when I reread the contract. For example, this contract is for a Hereford cow, but I believe you told me you actually bought a polled Hereford cow."

"Polled just means a Hereford that doesn't have any horns. It's the same thing."

"I have to disagree with you there. Under the law, Herefords and polled Herefords are two very distinct breeds. You run the risk of losing your pedigree unless we *insist* that they amend this contract."

"I'm sure Lester didn't know."

"If that's true, then they'll have no objection to signing all the additional papers I'm enclosing, just to make sure."

"Okay, I just want this to be over."

"And so do I," says the lawyer. "I know it's frustrating, but I'm protecting you against a whole lot of hassles later."

And so the letter, contract, riders, and amendments are all sent over to Lester's lawyer. Lester's lawyer takes four days to review them, then writes a memo to Lester that begins: "Based on the additional terms and conditions proposed by the recent purchaser of your livestock, I must recommend that you put the $600 check for the purchase price in escrow until this matter is resolved." And then Lester's lawyer proposes a formal registered-letter response to the other lawyer's formal registered letter.

Lester is confused. He's already spent the $600, he tells the lawyer.

"In that case," the lawyer tells him, "our position should be that our obligation to the buyer no longer exists, the sale is complete and final, and we are not required to make any amendments to the contract."

"What amendments do they want?"

"They want the cow listed as a polled Hereford instead of a Hereford."

"Did that rascal cut her horns off?"

"As I understand it, the plaintiffs are claiming that the animal was hornless at the time of sale."

"May of been. I don't recall."

"In that case, we'll write a simple one-paragraph registered letter stating that we will no longer respond to any demands made by the plaintiff, and that furthermore, we can't verify that the transferred animal was hornless or horned at the time of transfer."

"That's fine with me."

"Of course, the matter of the thirty-day no-resell clause is still unresolved. That might require a separate action."

"That's true."

"I'll tell you what, Lester. Maybe if I called the other lawyer, we could hash this out on the phone. I wouldn't agree to anything without your approval, of course."

"That's a good idea. Yall hash it out on the phone."

And so Lester's lawyer calls the other lawyer. The other lawyer is out, of course. Two days later the other lawyer calls back. Lester's lawyer is in court that day. Three days later, after Lester's lawyer's trial is over, he calls the other lawyer back. The other lawyer is out again, so he arranges a telephone appointment through the other lawyer's legal assistant. The telephone appointment is set for the following Tuesday.

At the appointed time, on the following Tuesday, the two lawyers argue for forty-five minutes about the thirty-day no-resell clause, the distinction between a Hereford and a polled Hereford, the ethics of spending the $600 before the final contract was signed, and other issues that occur to them in the course of the conversation. At the end of the conversation, they have reached a tentative agreement to resolve the conflicts by a "mutual cessation of hostilities."

Both lawyers call their clients the next day and explain what a "mutual cessation of hostilities" is.

Lester's lawyer says, "What it means is that they would agree to drop their claim that the animal is actually a polled Hereford. In return, we would drop our demand for the thirty-day no-resell clause."

"That's fine with me," says Lester.

"We're really getting the better deal," the lawyer explains. "Because three weeks have already passed, so there are only seven days left on the thirty-day no-resell period anyway."

And the other lawyer is saying, "We would really be getting the best of this deal, because they have to drop their claim entirely, but we can get what we want. If that animal is actually a genetic polled Hereford, we can have an independent veterinarian make that determination and certify it *regardless* of what papers we've signed. So I would recommend making this deal."

"Fine," says the buyer.

A week later, the formal agreement for a "mutual cessation of hostilities" is drawn up by Lester's lawyer and sent to Lester for his approval. Lester signs it without reading it. It's sent by registered mail to the other lawyer, who, after a delay of four business days, forwards it to the buyer of the cow.

The following day, the cow dies from a single gunshot fired directly into the back of its brain. No one can be sure who did it.

We can be certain it wasn't a lawyer.

DESIGNER HIPPIES

Have you heard about these guys that changed from raving sixties radicals to froth-mouth nineties Republicans? It's true. David Horowitz, Peter Collier, and a whole bunch of Che Guevara Communist hippie Freaksters from *Ramparts* magazine that wear wire-rim glasses and never comb their hair are *listening to Paul Harvey on the radio*. And then they sit around and have rap sessions about how "You know, Mr. Harvey has the soul of the common man in his bones." And then they all go to a country-western bar and do the cotton-eyed Joe with girls named Velma.

Meanwhile, these guys are being taken *seriously* by the Bush people. They're putting out newspapers and organizing think tanks and setting up offices in Washington and writing speeches for congressmen that want to fund the Stealth bomber with Grandma's Medicare checks. They're having a contest to see who can marry Fawn Hall and talk her into fathering eight or nine document-shredding children.

So how did they manage this anyhow?

Evidently they used the same excuse I used to tell my mama when I was nine years old: "I didn't *mean* it."

Like remember the time they marched to Washington and spray-painted KILL ALL FASCIST PIGS on the steps of the Supreme Court?

They didn't really *mean* it. They were *feeling bad* that day. They were having *personal problems* at home. In fact, one of their closest friends died that week. If it hadn't been such a, like, you know, weird week, they would have written something like SUPPORT YOUR LOCAL POLICE and then left twenty bucks on the step for the government's cleaning expenses.

All you guys that took that so seriously, and started spray-painting city halls all across America, don't you have minds of your own? What do you do, go around *copying* people who have medical and personal problems?

Or what about that time they called on all the black students at Tennessee State University to arm themselves, barricade themselves in their dorm rooms, and refuse to go to class, because the revolution was coming that spring? What about bringing Stokely Carmichael to town right at the moment the students were ready to surge out into the streets and blow away establishment pinstripe-suited weasel-face college deans?

Well, you see, they didn't *mean* it. They just kinda got excited, and they were young, and it was spring—you know how spring can make you crazy?—and there was this really foxy black girl that was leading the guys over at TSU and she was, like, so *exotic*, and we just got carried away.

And then there was the Greenwich Village underground hideout and crash house for draft evaders heading for Canada. Yeah, they knew about it, they helped out, sure, but they didn't think those guys would *really* break the law. I mean, when you're in elementary school, you talk about burning down the school, but you don't *do it*. Some of those guys really went to Canada, sure, but now that we're all right-thinking nineties Republicans, maybe we can bring them all to justice and, like, shoot em or something.

And you'd probably like an explanation about all those plans they had to make America Communist and nationalize General Motors and offer free medical care to everyone and turn all the farms into organic co-ops. And you might be wondering how they could go to North Vietnam in 1970 and talk on Radio Hanoi about what a wonderful model society they have over there, and how America should be more like North Vietnam.

Well, there's a perfectly good explanation for that, too.

You see, they got kind of carried away on the Communism deal. We're really talking about semantics here. It wasn't really "Communism" with a capital *C* they were calling for, it was more like little-*c* "communism." What they were saying, really, is that we needed more justice in America. Yeah, justice, that's right—more justice in America, and the way to *get* it was communism, only now we wouldn't call it communism, we would call it . . . what's the word? . . . oh yeah, consumerism. So what they were talking about was *consumerism*. People *thought* it was communism, and that's why the Radio Hanoi thing happened. But see, you don't really understand that, either, because now we all go to the Vietnam Veterans Monument along with everybody else and it makes us cry, too. In fact, we should probably send some troops over there and kick North Vietnam's behind.

To which I say, Would someone please stick these loonies back on the Marin County herb farm that grew em? They've really only got one problem. They talk too much.

WOMEN OF THE WORLD,

PLEASE TURN BACK

BEFORE IT'S TOO LATE!

"Hey, Joe Bob, how come there aren't more women in your business?"

Whenever ladies ask me this, I don't know if I'm being attacked, like I'm doing something to keep female writers out, or whether they're saying, "Do you think if I wore a real short skirt and a sweater two sizes too little, I might get a job doing what you do?"

And the answers are:

1. There have always been plenty of great female writers.
2. Nope. The only places where a real short skirt helps out are radio and real estate.

"So how come there don't *seem* to be that many women writers?"

This is real simple to me. I don't know why you gals have never figured it out:

Because they're too *intelligent* to keep doing the same thing for thirty years like the men do.

I'll give you an example. Man starts out when he's nineteen years old, writing about high school sports. Now most people can only endure high school sports for about, oh, two weeks. But this is a *male* doing it, and so he writes about high school sports for five years. Then he wins an award. Uh-oh! Hide his typewriter! Whoops, too late! He decides that he's the greatest writer on high school sports in the history of the world, and so now he's gonna make a giant leap in his career—to *college* sports. He writes about this subject for the next *ten* years. It doesn't matter that, as time goes on, he can't remember which team is which, who won the Rose Bowl six years ago, or why he was interested in college sports in the first place. It's his *identity*. He gets *attention* for this. He stays up till two in the morning studying punt-return statistics. He forgets his wife's birthday. He sends out for Burger King nine or ten times a week. Why? Because he's a *writer*. He's proud. He's professional. He's talented. Thousands of people read his words every day. Thirty-five years later, he's still doing the same thing, only now he has a daily column. And maybe he'll die happy, like Grantland Rice, the legendary sportswriter who simply slumped over his typewriter one day *in the press box!*

Now let's look at the female. She's nineteen years old, writing about high school sports. Except she's different from the male. She doesn't go to the ball game and think, "How can I write this so that everybody will think how good it is and read my byline at the top?" She's thinking "That's *very* interesting the way he did a 360-degree turn in midair and slam-dunked the ball." And so she writes a great story, describing the game, and everybody tells her, "Gee whiz, you're talented. You should cover professional basketball. Maybe you should have a column. You know, there aren't enough women in this business." And she says, "That's very nice, but I don't think I could watch men doing slam-dunks for a living every night of the week."

What!!!!! Are you kidding! She would *throw away* this budding career?

"I think maybe I would have more fun writing about crime."

What!!!!! You're ruining your career! You're crazy!

And so she goes and writes about crime for a while, and she does such a good job that she gets a book contract, and the book comes out and gets great reviews, and someone tells her, "Boy, have you got it made now. You can write *crime books* the rest of your life. There's big money in that. There's never been a great woman crime-book writer, someone on the level of Truman Capote."

And she says, "I didn't say I wanted to just do *that* my whole life."

And the editor says, "Well, you're such a good writer, you could probably work in any area you chose."

And she says, "I was thinking of going back to school, or maybe sailing around the world."

And he goes *through the roof!* "*What?!* Don't you realize . . . blah blah blah."

Because the women who are good at this are the ones who do it because they enjoy the *work*, not the *career*. If you ask a woman you haven't seen for ten years, "How's the work going? I remember you were doing stained-glass windows the last time I saw you"—she's liable to say, "Oh, I stopped doing that, I got tired of it." But if you ask a man about his stamp collection, which he hasn't *opened* for twenty years, he'll say, "Yes, I'm still doing that—I'm gonna get *right* back to it next week." And he's not lying to you. He's lying to himself. The man thinks if he doesn't do the same thing the rest of his life, following his first article with a second, and a third, and a book, and a second book, and on and on, then he's *wasting his life*. A woman thinks that doing the exact same thing the rest of her life is boring, and, in fact, *that* is wasting your life.

Fortunately, now that "career women" have penetrated into every area of American society, they have the opportunity to be just as miserable as us men. And I, for one, welcome it, because I was thinking of sailing around the world.

THIS CHAPTER SPONSORED

BY TACO BELL

T he other day I met this guy who didn't have a corporate sponsor yet. His name was Jimbo.

"Jimbo what?" I asked him.

"Jimbo Jeffreys."

"No, I mean your full name. What is it? Jimbo 'Bud Lite' Jeffreys? Texaco Jimbo Jeffreys? Or maybe you have one of those fancy names, like 'The Prudential Jimbo Jeffreys Living Human Unit.'"

"Nope," he told me, "just Jimbo Jeffreys."

So I thought I'd let you know that there's one thing left in America that doesn't have a corporate sponsor. I read in the paper where there's a college football team out in San Diego that's gonna have a sponsor for all their home games—the San Diego State Wheaties, or something like that—and then I read about a couple guys in New York that are publishing books with ads in every chapter:

"She was slinky and luscious, with a lower lip that stuck out two inches and a bundle of blond hair that could kill. She stood in the doorway, beckoning with her eyes. 'I think we should do a little *work* together,' she said, but the way she said 'work' made the hair on the back of my neck stand up. I stubbed out my cigarette on the desk and then I stared at her for a long long time, and she stared right back, and then—Preparation H takes the sting out of nagging hemorrhoids—suddenly I had no interest in her anymore."

A couple months ago John McEnroe came to town for the World Championship Tennis finals—which I think is the Mitsubishi World Championship Tennis finals, or something like that—and he'd rented out every inch of his tennis clothes *and* his racket. If you watched him real close, when he served, there was an ad for Burger King in each armpit. There's even a whole set of tennis tournaments called the Virginia Slims. That's it. That's the whole name. Virginia Slims. The geniuses who thought this up decided the same people who admire Martina Navratilova's awesome forehand would also say, "You know what, if the tennis tournament is this good, I think I'll stick one of those *cigarettes* in my mouth, too!"

"Yeah, they must be good. They're named after a tennis tournament!"

"Yeah, they must be good *for* you, too."

A friend of mine named Shirley Stubbs got pregnant last year and wanted to have her baby at the Grapevine Hospital in Grapevine, Texas. Only it's not the Grapevine Hospital anymore. It's the Squibb-Teledyne-Merck Medical Center. When the baby was born, they immediately gave him a little plastic bag full of dental-care products, diaper-service coupons, a Louisville Slugger, and catalogs from three universities. Then she had *another* baby, and a guy from Xerox showed up to talk about endorsements.

Another guy I know named Neville Gitchell—he used to be Stan Gitchell, but he changed it when he went to Hollywood—he's an actor who always wanted to be Hamlet in Shakespeare-in-the-Park. That was the first year he was an actor. The second year he was an actor he wanted to make love to Meryl Streep in the movies. Now all he ever says is, "You know what? If I could just get *one* good Löwenbräu commercial, I think my career would really take off."

I've been trying to figure out just exactly what's going on here. Like this year I went to the Cotton Bowl, which is now the Mobil Cotton Bowl, and the whole game I kept looking at the fifty-yard line where it said MOBIL COTTON BOWL on top of a drawing of a cotton boll, and I was thinking to myself, "When exactly is this piece of advertising supposed to kick in on me?" I mean, you couldn't really buy any Mobil products at the Cotton Bowl game. Would it be on the freeway going home? Would I suddenly say, "Oh yeah, I need gas. Let's see, I was just at the Cotton Bowl. . . . Gas, Cotton Bowl, gas, Cotton Bowl . . . Mobil! That's what I need! A Mobil station!" You see what I'm getting at here? Or is it that Mobil wants to be connected in my mind to the game of football? Let's say I'm sitting in a La-Z-Boy recliner flipping through *Sports Illustrated*, and all of a sudden I see a picture of Troy Aikman, who played in the Cotton Bowl. Is it lodged back there in my brain somewhere, so that I'm thinking, "Troy Aikman, Troy Aikman, UCLA, Cotton Bowl,

Mobil Cotton Bowl," and suddenly I scream out "Wanda! Would you go fill my car up at the Mobil station?"

In other words, I don't get it. I understand why the Cotton Bowl does it. They want the jack. I understand why John McEnroe does it. He probly gets about a hundred thou per armpit. I understand why Neville Gitchell wants to be in a fifteen-second Löwenbräu commercial instead of a three-hour version of *Hamlet*—because Gitchell never did wanna be an actor in the first place. He just wanted to be *famous*. But I don't understand what Mobil gets out of it, unless there are people out there that are saying, "Oh yeah, Mobil. They *must* have good stuff because they're famous. I *hear* about em all the time."

"What do you hear about em?"

"I don't know. I just hear about em."

I think this is what Mobil believes. This is what the ad agencies have sold em for the big bucks. I've lived in America all my life, and I think they're probly wrong. But you know what I think we should do?

Don't tell em it's not *working*.

Maybe we can all get some money out of it.

A KINDER, GENTLER DRUG

The new drug for the nineties, as proclaimed on the cover of *Newsweek,* is the little green-and-white "happy capsule" called Prozac. Feeling depressed? Lost your job? Lost your spouse? Lost your wallet? Lost your cable TV?

Pop a Prozac! You get your job back. You get a new spouse. You become a millionaire. . . . Wait a minute. That can't be right. Let's see . . .

Pop a Prozac! You still don't have a job, but you feel *great* about not having a job. Your wife is living with a lesbian in Aspen, but you suddenly *love* lesbians. You start considering lesbianism as a career option. The repo man is outside, hooking up a tow truck to your Isuzu. You run out of the house and help him adjust the winch.

Now don't think this is some kind of new Valium drug. Valium is so *eighties*. Valium makes you mellow. Valium makes you wanna move to Oregon. Prozac is something entirely different. Prozac turns you into a Frequent Flyer. Prozac pumps so much energy into you that you go to Tokyo and apply for a computer-programming job at Sony. Prozac gets you out of your dingy apartment and into the President's Health Spa Super Weight-Training Circuit. As soon as you take Prozac, you wanna go to Beirut and liberate the hostages.

What's going on here?

This stuff is about a buck-sixty *per hit*. It would be more economical just to use cigarettes and coffee.

But people swear by this drug:

"I used to wash my underwear nine times a day. Sometimes I would have to wash my underwear in public fountains, just so I could be certain that it remained washed. Then I discovered Prozac. Now I only wash my underwear three times a day."

"I had ninety-seven jobs in three years. I was starting to worry that I was simply unemployable. Then I tried Prozac. Now nobody will hire me, because I can't pass the drug test, so I *don't have to worry about it anymore.*"

"I always dreamed of being a ballerina. When I was turned down by the Royal Danish Ballet, I was devastated. I thought they should have given me some reason other than my age. But all they said was, 'We aren't hiring fifty-six-year-old dancers.' You can imagine my feelings of rage, of inadequacy. If I hadn't found Prozac, I'm sure I would have either firebombed the place or cut off my legs. Or both. But now I have no desire to mutilate anything except my neighbor's cat."

So, you see, a lot of what this is is taking people who are already ready for Looney Tunes—and making em a *little less* looney. So you're taking somebody who's spent the last ten years trying to stick a square peg in a round hole, and so they're frustrated. You tell em to pop a Prozac. They keep trying to stick the same square peg in the same round hole, but now *they think it's going in.*

Do you see the beauty here? Instead of saying something like, "Well, you hate that job, you shouldn't even *have* that job," they say "Well, you hate that job, but *here!* Take one of *these!* Now you don't hate the job anymore. You can do it for thirty more years and never even realize what you're doing."

We had a lot easier solution out in West Texas. Most towns didn't have a psychiatrist, but we always had a preacher. And so you'd go to the preacher and tell whatever your long, complicated problem was, like, "The ranch foreman's been hasslin me, and they're saying that if the cotton fails then the migrant workers might not show up this year and my wife'll get laid off at the elementary school and my truck threw a rod and it's gonna cost me 250 bucks and . . ."

And it didn't matter how long this stuff would go on, the preacher would always just say, "Leon, stop thinking about yourself."

And then Leon would start in again: "Well, I guess I am kinda wrought up over this, but I don't know where the money's gonna come from for the truck, that's probly the number-one problem. . . ."

And then the preacher would say, "Leon, you don't need a truck. You wanted to talk to me today, so you got your hiney over here without a truck, didn't you?"

"Well, yessir, that's true," Leon would say, "but this problem of the wife gettin laid off means . . ."

"Leon," the preacher would interrupt, "she's *not* laid off, is she? That's something in your own head, isn't it? Because you're real busy thinking about yourself."

"Well, sir, I just don't know what we'd do if . . ."

"Leon, you just show up over here at the church any day you feel like it, and I'll *give* you something to do. You're not worried about not having anything to do. You're worried about not getting to do just exactly what you wanna do, no matter what."

"Well, yessir, I guess that's true. But the foreman's been giving me a hard time and . . ."

"Leon, we can do this two ways. You can stop thinking about yourself, put your eyes on somebody else, like your wife. You're not doing her a bit of good, moonin around like this. Or me. You're wastin *my* time, Leon, cause I got people that are really in trouble, really sick, in jail, and you're coming in here telling me stuff you're dreaming up in your head about *yourself.* So you can stop it, or you can go home and lock the door and just think about yourself so much and so hard that eventually your head will explode and then the next time I see you you'll be begging me to make your headache and your ulcer go away, and you know what I'll say to you then, Leon?"

"Stop thinking about myself?"

"Stop thinking about yourself. That's right. It works cause you wanna do it, and it works cause you *haveta* do it, but it always works."

"Oh."

"And on your way home, Leon . . ."

"Yessir."

"Rake some leaves for Miz Carruthers. She's got arthritis."

"Yessir."

"You feel better, don't you?"

"Yessir."

Of course, it's too bad we didn't have Prozac in West Texas. We could have saved the preacher a lot of time.

THE W-WORD

L ately I've been having nightmares about "womanizing." This is the new word all the newscast-
ers use when they're trying to say "Hey! Look at this guy! He's
a sorry piece of leftover donut! Look how narrow his eyes are!
Make sure your daughters are in the house if *this guy* shows
up!" You remember how John Tower got turned down for secretary of defense? Everybody forgot exactly what it was he was
accused of, but every time he showed his face in public, they
beaned him with the W-word.

Shoot, why do you think Texans voted for the guy all those
years? We didn't even know it was a *crime*. We thought John
showed excellent judgment in most of the gals he sashayed
around with. And, besides, she *already left him*. He was *di-*

vorced. It was *over*. He was *single* when all this stuff was going on. Even if he did do the *W*-sin while married, it was obviously a marriage that was going straight into the toilet. So what's the big deal if the guy cats around D.C. a little bit?

So anyway, I've been having these nightmares about what would happen if I woke up one day and somebody appointed me to the government.

"Of course, Mr. Briggs, you realize that you will have to undergo a routine FBI sex investigation."

And then in the next part of the dream I'm shaking, sweating, moaning as they haul me in front of the Senate confirmation committee.

"Mr. Briggs, we have here a sworn affidavit from Floyce Struthers, who was employed at the Le Bodine hairstyling salon from March 1974 until February 1975. Do you recall this as being correct?"

"I swear it was nothing! Nothing! Well, maybe one time, but I *called* her the next day. I know she says I didn't call her, but I *called* her."

"Do you recall this statement, Mr. Briggs? Do you recall saying 'You weren't anything like I expected'? Did you indeed say that on the afternoon following said encounter?"

"Lies! Lies!"

"Mr. Briggs, we have serious allegations of womanizing here."

"But I was ridden with guilt for *days* after that."

"I'm sorry, sir. Womanizing is womanizing."

"What if Floyce Struthers was man-izing?"

"Our next line of questioning, Mr. Briggs, involves one Susan Caravaggio, who was in the audience at the Lotta Laffs Comedy Club in Terre Haute, Indiana, on the evening of April 10, 1986."

"Yes, she was, but nothing happened."

"Miss Caravaggio has stated that you offered to buy her twelve drinks after the show."

"It was strictly a business expense. I frequently buy drinks for members of the audience. Public relations."

"Do you recall her stating that you were attempting to intoxicate her so that you could do some *womanizing?*"

"Yes sir, but she got sick first. I'm clean on this one."

"Mr. Briggs, I hardly think it matters that the woman was physically unable to consummate said womanizing. The intent to womanize is quite clear."

"But I didn't *do* anything. She didn't even *want* to do anything."

"In that case, I'll seek opinion of counsel as to whether attempting to womanize but being rebuffed by the victim of womanization constitutes actual womanizing or a lesser offense."

"Clean as a whistle on that one. You know her nickname, don't you? They called her Welcome-Wagon Caravaggio."

"Just answer the questions, Mr. Briggs."

"I'm sorry, sir. If I had known these were going to be crimes in the year 1991, I would have thought twice about my behavior."

"Well, you should have thought of that a *long time ago*, shouldn't you?"

"Yessir."

"We have one final case here. It involves Heather 'the Snake' Felson of Boston. Do you recall meeting this woman?"

"She's a stripper. Works the Combat Zone. I saw her show. Works with a boa constrictor. And I know what you're gonna say. But it's not what you think. She came over and sat at my table. We talked. She left. That was it."

"And what did you talk about?"

"As I recall, we discussed the Boston Red Sox."

"Wasn't she, in fact, on the payroll of the Boston Red Sox at that time?"

"Not to my knowledge."

"Wasn't she, in fact, considered a favorite of several of the Boston Red Sox players?"

"No, I would say she was two or three down the list."

"Wasn't she, in fact, known around Boston for one thing and one thing only?"

"All right! All right! I admit it! You caught me! One time! Once in my life! I did it! I *womanized*! I womanized all night long! I womanized so long I couldn't walk for three days! And do you know what? I'm glad I womanized! I loved womanizing! I would do it again if I wasn't going to jail for it. I hate you nonwomanizing people! You're sick!"

"Bailiff! Bailiff!"

At this point the dream dissolves as four armed guards carry me out of the Senate chamber screaming.

These new people they got in D.C. are *scary*.

HOW WALL STREET WORKS

I t's times like this, when the Dow Jones Industrial Hoo-Haws are zipping toward a zillion and the whole world is buying up America, that idiots like me decide to invest in the stock market.

We don't know any better.

Sure, we know what you're gonna say. We watch Louis Rukeyser, too. (Get a new couch, Louie!) "Buy low, sell high." Sure, sure, sure. We know, we know, we know. But we can't *do* it. Something's seriously wrong with us. Everybody in New York is waiting for the dufus from Grapevine, Texas, to plunk his three hundred dollars down on the table. Then a guy on the floor of the Stock Exchange will scream, "Joe Bob's buying! Joe

Bob's buying!" and you'll hear a thousand voices yelling "Sell!"
and "Put!" and "People in Grapevine, Texas, are in this deal!
Get out! Get out!"

And do you know why this is?

Because every one of em went to the same "Investing for the
Coming Depression" seminar, and the first thing they told em
was, "When you see the checks pouring in from the wheat fields
of Iowa and the fishing shacks of Mississippi, take all your
money out of the market and put it in a mattress."

People like me—people that don't really have any business
getting into the stock market—are a warning to Wall Street big
shots. We're what they call "uneducated money." And once the
uneducated money gets in there, all the stocks get overvalued,
and then everybody in Trump Plaza starts getting nervous, and
then some Japanese guys in Tokyo start taking their money out
of New York and buying Doitchie Marks with it, and then three
savings and loans in New Jersey fail, and then countries in Latin
America start having revolutions, and then everybody *really*
gets nervous, because if the drug dealers take *their* money out,
then we're all done. Crash City. Window jumpers. Suddenly
people in Los Angeles have to sell their houses for only 100
percent more than they paid for them.

Nah, on second thought, I guess it could *never* get that bad.

Fortunately, I've been boning up this time. I've been reading
Money magazine and *Your Money* magazine and *Money Manager* magazine and *Gimme One of Them Hundred Dollar Bills*
magazine. And here's what I've figured out that'll save all us
idiots in the sticks from certain financial disaster.

1. Invest only in stocks you've never heard of, with names
   that put you into a coma. Let's say you find this stock
   called Unimark National. Perfect name. It's so boring

you're forced to take a fifteen-minute nap every time you say it. Unimark. Unimark National. There's no way you'll ever even *remember* it. This makes it a perfect Wall Street stock. It's the opposite of what your friends have been saying, right? They've been saying, "You know what? I believe I'll get me some of that Wal-Mart stock. There's always *thousands* of people in that store when I go in there." And so, of course, they put their money in something they *understand*, along with 19 million other people with the same idea, and pretty soon they don't *have* their money anymore. That's why *you* are going to follow my second principle. . . .

2. Invest only in stocks engaged in a business you can't figure out. Let's say Unimark National makes industrial connector pipe for hydroelectric dams. That's a very good business. It's boring, it's necessary, and very few people understand it. But let's go a step farther. Let's say Unimark National makes the computer software for the company that *designs* the industrial connector pipe for hydroelectric dams. This is a *great* stock to buy. It's so obscure that even the people who use it don't know what it is. (By the way, any stock with "software" somewhere in the description is perfect. "Software" means they don't really have *anything* to sell, but they've figured out how to sell it to people who don't know what "software" is.) But there's even a *better* Unimark National stock to buy. Let's say Unimark National is a business consultant to companies who design software for industrial connector pipe used in hydroelectric dams. This means they don't have anything to do with the dam, the pipe, or the software, but they're the only people in the project who *can't be fired*! Isn't American business great?

3. Finally, invest in a company that has recently been accused of insider trading, commercial bribery, investing in South Africa, embezzlement, extortion, or preferably a combination of all of the above. Of course, the people who did the actual crimes have been sent away, and the company now claims it's squeaky clean, but, meanwhile, all the Wall Street guys have deserted the stock. Why? They feel so guilty about their *own* deals all the time that they think a) the charges *must be true*, and b) sooner or later, the company's gonna get caught and put out of business. Did you see how all the financial vultures jumped on Leona Helmsley like she was the first human being in history to cheat on her taxes?

Meanwhile, us idiots out here in the sticks, who pay our taxes and don't understand what insider trading is, simply notice that the stock is *undervalued*. It's a definite buy. Or, as Louie Rukeyser would put it, "Suddenly the bulls are running in Texas."

CRUEL AND UNUSUAL DAY CARE

I didn't realize until this past year that I had a stunted, unhappy, unnatural childhood development. My mama *worked* all the time.

Of course, we didn't know you weren't supposed to do this. We didn't read all the polls in *Newsweek* and the Sunday feature articles on "Guilt and the Working Mother" and studies by the National Opinion Research Center that say "the intellectual development of boys from middle-income homes slows if they are cared for by others during infancy while their mothers hold down a full-time job."

We didn't know any of this.

If we'd ever said any of this stuff to Mama, who was a schoolteacher, she would have said "Oh my goodness!" She would have *believed* it. And then she would have probly taken away our favorite baby-sitters and the right to play in the neighbors' backyards and especially the right to spend all day at Miz Samuels's house chunkin rocks at squirrels. This would be called "day care" now. Miz Samuels got about twenty bucks a week for it. We just called it spending all day at Miz Samuels's house chunkin rocks at squirrels.

If Mama would have ever come home and said, "Come on, let's spend some Quality Time together!" we would have said, "Do we *have* to? I want to ride my bike over to Ernie's." And so, of course, we robbed ourselves of all that Quality Time, and we're probly pitiful human beings as a result.

When you read this stuff today in the newspapers about how working mothers are neglecting their kids, it sounds like they dump the little yard monsters off at some Nazi concentration camp with barbed-wire fence and then drive away while their little pink noses are sticking through the wire and they bawl and whine and say, "But, Mommy, I want *you!*"

We were so maladjusted that as soon as we would roll up in front of the day-care woman's house, we'd pop the doors on the car open before the car ever rolled to a stop. "Don't forget your . . ."

But we'd already be *inside the house*, getting out the Spalding punching bag that her nephew Kevin got for Christmas.

". . . coat," Mama would say, sitting in the car by herself.

And then she would carry the coat up to the front door and tell Miz Samuels, "If you ever have any trouble with them, you have my permission to do whatever is necessary."

Of course, we all knew what that meant. It meant, "You just whale the tar out of em anytime you feel like it." This was for occasions like the time me and Radley Stone tried to snap the head off a snake by cracking it like a whip. It was something the Scoutmaster told us about. He *claimed* it could be done, that there were cowboys a hundred years ago who could do it. So we both got beat on for a few minutes. In today's day-care system, the solution would be to "talk to your parents." But we had the mentality of pet cocker spaniels: If you didn't punish us *right when we did it*, then we'd forget about it and, when you tried to punish us later, we wouldn't know why we were being punished. Ever once in a while, we would have a day-care lady who didn't have the intestinal fortitude to threaten physical abuse. So later in the day, when we finally got whistled down for whatever capital crime we committed, we'd get real *resentful*, like, "So why are you bringing that up now?" In other words, we'd become *more* obnoxious. So quick and summary punishment tended to be the only thing that would work.

But the main thing you have to remember is that Mama was always afraid that *we* would gang up on Miz Samuels. It was like, when Mama drove away from the Nazi compound, it was the day-care woman who had *her* face pushed up against the bars, whimpering, wondering when Mama would come back and make her feel better about her life.

If we ever wondered where Mama was during all that time— which we would, occasionally, when we got *real* bored—we'd be told, "At the school."

And this satisfied us.

This was a sufficient answer.

Of course, today, in order to be completely honest with a kid, you would have to say, "Pursuing her own selfish career goals."

To which we would have said, "What?"

We wouldn't understand that. We would have changed the

subject. We would have said, "Mama, can we have a baby-sitter this weekend?"

"Yall are too old for a baby-sitter."

(The baby-sitters stopped when she realized one day that I could possibly have a sexual interest in junior-high girls. We still begged for continuing adult supervision.)

We were a weird, maladjusted family. Because, without knowing exactly why we knew what we knew, we kids understood that it never mattered where Mama was or how much Quality Time she spent with us or exactly what day-care house she left us in or what she did for a living or how often she used a baby-sitter. All that mattered was that Mama was Mama.

DESIGNER GENES II

There's a professor at Harvard, guy named Herrnstein, who says the quality of babies is going way
down. I've noticed this myself. If you've been around any babies
lately, you've probly seen the obvious lack of intelligence. Most
of em want the rattle that's lying on the floor instead of the one
in their hand. Then, when you give em the one on the floor, they
throw it *back* on the floor. So you can see, I'm sure, the point
Professor Herrnstein is making. The *wrong people* are having
babies!

You know who's having babies? Women with low IQs. Your
airhead bimbos are domino-ing like crazy.

And who's *not* having babies? Women with high IQs and

plenty of money to get tubular-occlusion-litigation surgery or whatever it's called, the deal where you basically tell the doctor, "Just keep cuttin on me till the baby-maker is all gummed up."

And what Dr. Herrnstein is saying is that, by the year 2000, if this keeps up, we aren't gonna have enough parts in sitcoms for all the people in America who aren't fit for any other job. In other words, the gene pool is petering out. The only people having babies are topless-bar owners and backhoe operators. And those babies are just not up to snuff.

Have you ever noticed how this new crop of babies will grab a man's glasses and rip em off his face for no reason? These are *aggressive* babies. How about the number of times they interrupt important conversations with remarks that are completely *off the subject*? Obviously, they are *rude* babies. And probly the most disturbing thing of all is, when you send these new babies off to Baby School to start getting them ready to go to Harvard, all they wanna do is eat their coloring books.

I'm not even gonna go into the table-manners situation.

Obviously, something's got to be done. Dr. Herrnstein suggests that big law firms and stock brokerages and banks and universities should encourage real *smart* women employees to stay at home and have babies—and let em do all their work on the kitchen table. I'm sure that Dr. Herrnstein has studied the situation and so he knows that, since these are extremely *intelligent* babies these women will be having, they won't be pounding their fists on the home-computer keyboard and accidentally buying 12,000 Eurodollar futures contracts on the Tokyo exchange for Mommy.

The second thing we should do is pay for abortions for the poor. Dr. Herrnstein says a lot of these *stupid* ladies really want abortions, but they just can't afford em. And let's face it, if they had a baby, it would probly be one of those that spits up all the time and refuses to hold its left arm up so it can be strapped in the car seat. I mean, does society really need that type of individual?

The third thing the professor wants to do is change the tax exemptions, so that the richer you are, the more money you take off your taxes every time you give birth. You see the beauty here?

"You know what, honey? I've been thinking about having a baby."

"That's great! Let me call Sal down at Merrill Lynch tomorrow morning, we'll work out the numbers, check the tax situation, and see if it's feasible in this fiscal year."

And finally, Dr. Herrnstein wants to cut off all welfare payments that are based on the number of kids you have. In other words, a lot of these people are having baby after baby after baby just so they can get rich. Every time they have a kid—whap!—fifty bucks a week! And they don't have to *do anything* for that money! They're just sitting around, surrounded by all these low-IQ babies, collecting that money, not even *concerned* that their babies are so stupid and unambitious that most of em sleep twelve hours a day and spend the rest of their time trying to ride the cat like a horse.

Obviously, we need to do something now. Dr. Herrnstein says we're losing one IQ point every year that these American smart people decide to get triple-bypass vasectomy surgery. In fact, earlier this year I was in Cambridge, Massachusetts, the city where Dr. Herrnstein works, and I noticed the problem is a whole lot worse than we thought. Cambridge is a city that mainly attracts people who think they're smart. The main way they feel self-respect is through their intelligence. So, you see, there's an entire city brimming with people who are so out of touch with America that they despise everything the rest of us stand for. Too bad we didn't have government-sponsored abortions for their parents. America would be a happier place.

THE NEW BILL OF RIGHTS

Now that the Congress is talking about making a bunch of amendments to the Bill of Rights, I wanna suggest a few that ought to be in there, mainly because everybody *acts* like they're in there already.

1. The right to have a baby after the age of forty: This was passed at the insistence of aging soap-opera stars, who want the chance to describe every excruciating detail of their pregnancy, morning sickness, and childbirth to *People* magazine. In fact, since so many of them lie about their age, we better extend the baby-bearing years to at least fifty, with hardship exemptions for those women who "just didn't have time in my early career." These women should

be allowed to have children up to the age of eighty-six.
2. The right to say any idiotic thing that pops into your head on a radio talk show and *still be taken seriously*: This would put an end to the current crop of talk-show hosts who simply *hang up* on callers, causing the audience to get uneasy that someone's feelings were hurt. In fact, we need to pass . . .
3. The right to never have your feelings hurt: This would end the existence of *mean* people.
4. The right to keep all your money for yourself, no matter what taxes you owe, who else needs it, what city you live in, what benefits you get from the government, what medical problems you have, what investments you have or have not made, and how well you do your job, because "This is America."
5. The right to Nielsen ratings: This would avoid the sticky questions of how to choose church pastors, doctors, lawyers, accountants, mayors, city managers, airplane pilots, and maids. Simply send em to NBC Testing & Research, where a studio audience is wired up for its galvanic-skin-response reaction. Whoever gets at least a 20 rating and a 25 share is certified acceptable.
6. The right to own whatever house you "deserve": Are you having trouble getting a 250 percent balloon-payment loan at 4 percent interest so you can finally move out of that crummy apartment and get a five-bedroom with game room, lawn, pool, terrace, garden, and gazebo? Apparently you haven't been listening to our Congress talk about "the right to home ownership." It's yours. Go ahead. You can pay it back later. That's what the government does.
7. The right to cost-of-living adjustments to everything:

When inflation goes up, you get more money—exactly the amount that inflation went up. This has the added advantage of making inflation go up faster, which means you'll get even more money.

8. The right to never do laundry: Laundry is something people did for themselves in an earlier era of American history. Today we have illegal aliens and below-minimum-wage teenagers to do it for us. That also applies to lawn-mowing, all cooking except barbecues, and home repair. People who don't have money for hired help to come over and fix the microwave will now get government grants for that purpose.

9. The right to get a bunch of interest on your money but rip it out of the bank whenever you want to.

And, finally:

10. The right to get mad and kick any politician out of office who's as greedy and selfish as we are.

These are already in effect, but we should go ahead and pass em into law, just for the record.

A couple days ago the University of Nevada–Las Vegas wasted Duke in the big hoo-haw NC double-A tournament, and, as the whole world knows, it was the biggest, most lopsided blowout of any championship game in history. Then everyone started acting like this should be humiliating to Duke. That's not the way I saw it. It should be humiliating to UNLV.

There's this one moment in the game I can't get out of my mind. I kept expecting some sportswriter to mention it, but nobody ever did.

It happened near the end of the game. The game was actually over with fifteen minutes left to play, but this was even later,

when Duke was totally demoralized, hanging their heads, trot-
ting up and down the court like robots. There were five minutes
left, and UNLV led the game, 90 to 59.

It was impossible for Duke to win the game. Not improbable.
Not a slim chance. Impossible.

And what do athletes normally do when a game is decided so
early? I've played on a few teams and coached a team of fourth-
graders. It's the same on every level from the church leagues to
the NBA. The winning team plays as conservatively as possible,
holding the ball, taking time off the clock, often passing up
lay-ups so that the game can end quickly, and mercifully, and
the opponent can't be humiliated. The losing team plays as hard
as it can, so that even the losing will have dignity. And the losing
team never lets its anger or disappointment show.

You might call this a charade. I call it a ritual that is worth
preserving. It's the way one team shows respect to another.

But this is not what happened with five minutes left and
UNLV leading 90 to 59. With plenty of time on the shot clock,
with plenty of chances to pass the ball, dribble the ball, hurry
the game along, with the exhausted Duke players hardly even
summoning the strength to raise their arms on defense . . . a
senior UNLV guard named Stacey Cvijanovich drilled a three-
point shot!

And then the guys on the bench started high-fiving on the
bench, like they had made an important statement by leading 93
to 59 instead of just a measly 90 to 59.

I thought the player would get yanked out of the game. I've
seen *eight-year-olds* benched for less. But this guy was a hero!

Then, as the teams were finishing out the game, the CBS
television announcers, Brent Musburger and Billy Packer,
started talking about how, even though eight of these UNLV

players had been suspended during the season for "infractions" (like not paying hotel bills), they would now have "new respect." And even though Jerry Tarkanian, their coach, had been found guilty of NCAA rules violations himself, he would now "find respect." Because he *won the game*! Because he had these guys out there slam-dunking and three-point-shooting and— what used to be the cardinal sin in amateur sports—running up the score.

Where did these guys go to school? Did they have mothers?

Maybe Brent, and Billy, and Jerry forgot that there's another way to do it.

They probly wouldn't have understood a coach like Harley Redin, if they'd met him. Harley Redin still holds the record for the longest winning streak in college sports. His women's basketball team, the Flying Queens of tiny Wayland Baptist College in Plainview, Texas, won 131 consecutive games in the 1950s. They were so famous that the school eventually bought them a private plane, so they could do exhibitions all over the country. They were even *flashier* than UNLV. Instead of doing warm-up drills before each game, they did a fifteen-minute Harlem Globetrotter–type show of dribbling and trick shots.

But the game that all the women on that famous team remember is the national AAU championship game in 1958, when their 131-game winning streak was on the line against Nashville Business College. Nashville Business opened a sizable lead on the Flying Queens in the first half, but Wayland battled back to within two points. Then, near the end of the game, Nashville Business made a huge surge, sank two crucial free throws, and took a five-point lead that was virtually insurmountable. Some of the Wayland players started crying and yelling at one another, disputing foul calls, throwing temper tantrums, as the championship was slipping away. With fifteen seconds left, the game was already lost, but Coach Redin called time-out anyway.

In the huddle he looked at the girls' tear-streaked faces and said, "I called time-out so I could tell you this. I want you to go back out there and lose. And I want you to lose with the same kind of class that you've won with for the past five years."

Players on the 1958 team still remember that moment as the most thrilling in their careers.

Of course, Coach Redin probly couldn't get a job today.

PART 2

OUR

SUPERNATURAL

BEINGS

LETTER TO THE AYATOLLAH

(Written the week after the Ayatollah Khomeini offered a million dollars to anyone who would kill novelist Salman Rushdie)

Dear Your Holy Weirdness Ayatollah Chow-Mein-ee:

How are things over in Tehran? I heard it's a drag trying to find X-rated cassettes over there. What are the chicks like? On TV they look real stressed-out.

Listen, I got a proposition for you. This guy Rushdie turned out to be a weenie. You put out the contract on him, he immediately cratered and apologized. So you put out a bigger contract on him, he dives into a foxhole. We'll never see the guy again, and that's no fun for you.

So here's what I suggest. I've been one of your biggest enemies for years. In fact, if I knew you were reading novels in English,

I could have put a whole chapter or two in my last one, being obnoxious about Mohammed, just to make sure you would see it. Because, let's face it, it takes my books *forever* to sell out that first printing. That's where I think we can help each other.

I would be proud to be on your hit list. It would be great publicity for me, number one, but it would also give you some speech material. First thing I would do is go on *Nightline* and put out a contract on *you.* Then you could find some little slimeball terrorist crudhead coward—like the guy that blew up the Pan Am plane—and give him a million bucks to kill me. But you don't have to worry about me pulling a Rushdie on you. In fact, I would give you thousands of opportunities to kill me.

Do you realize how easy it would be to get booked on the *A.M. Cleveland* show if I could be killed at any moment during the interview? *People Are Talking* in Minneapolis. *The Ira Joe Fisher Morning Show* in Cincinnati. Drive-time FM radio—guys named "Murphy in the Morning" in every major American city. You want publicity? *I* would give you the publicity you need. All you have to do is give me a specific list of sentences I could write that would be morally and religiously and personally offensive to you. I'm *extremely* skilled at being obnoxious. Just to give you an example, let's start with a few ideas I have that might get us to the negotiating table.

What if I said "Mohammed had cooties"? Does that work for you? Are any of your brain tumors kicking in when you hear that? Okay, how about this one?

"The Jews are always right."

You have to understand, I'm a simple guy. I tried to read Rushdie's book, but I couldn't figure out where the insults were. So give me a little time here.

"Jesus was better than Mohammed. Shoot, even Moses was

better than Mohammed. In fact, you could take one of your lesser disciples—like Bartholomew, who cares about Bartholomew—even *Bartholomew* was better than Mohammed."

How am I doing? Wait! I know!

"Women are smarter than Muslim men."

Are you starting to think I'm a dangerous blasphemer? Wait, I'm not finished.

"Mecca is a dump."

"Wilt Chamberlain was a better player than Kareem Abdul-Jabbar."

"The shah was a hell of a guy."

"Go ahead, one little cocktail before dinner won't hurt."

"Iraqis go to heaven, too."

"A lot of the fourteen-year-old boys with machine guns running around *jihad*-ing and fighting and dying for you are not very well-adjusted teenagers. Some of them hate your guts. I wanted you to know this."

"Due to the curvature of the earth, you guys have been praying in the *wrong* direction all your lives. I guess the joke's on you, huh?"

"Not many people realize it, but Mohammed was actually a dyslexic prophet. He got all these messages from God, but he *transposed* them in his head. God would send the message 'You shall have a single wife for many years,' but Mohammed would get all mixed up and it would come out, 'I will have many wives for one year each.' You can see the problems this kind of thing caused."

I hope I'm getting close now. I realize I can't expect you to accept one measly letter as worthy of death, but I'm willing to work as hard as I can to blaspheme on a global scale. I'm very serious about this. I can't think of a single person on the planet

I would rather have hating me than you. You see, you picked on a British guy. Now I'd like to see you pick on an American guy. Because we won't run and hide. Because we would *love* to make you prove just how powerful your God is. Do you get my drift?

Hang loose, I think we can deal.

Yours in sincere mockery,

Joe Bob Briggs, Grapevine, Texas, U.S.A.

THE ZIG ZIGLAR PATH

TO WISDOM

"Excuse me, but are you Mr. Ziglar?"

"I am, and God bless you."

"Zig Ziglar, the guy who wrote *See You at the Top, Confessions of a Happy Christian*, and *Secrets of Closing the Sale*?"

"I'm proud to say I've done everything the Lord promised me I *could* do."

"Well, I have a problem."

"If you *think* you have a problem, you *will* have a problem. I call that Garbage Dump Thinking. What do you *think* your problem is?"

"I don't have any arms."

"You know, 'don't have' are just not words in my vocabulary.

'Don't have' is just a way of saying 'don't *want* to have,' because if you *want* to have something, you *will* have that something. Everything you want is available to you."

"I want arms, but I don't have any arms."

"But you *can* have arms. I suspect that all you're suffering from is a poor self-image. Maybe your *appearance* has been ridiculed repeatedly by your friends and acquaintances. Maybe you've accepted that ridicule by *assuming* that the way they see you is the way you should see yourself."

"Actually nobody ever mentions it at all. Everyone acts like I *do* have arms."

"That's because they believe in you more than you believe in yourself, and I guarantee you, that's how miracles happen. Man was designed for accomplishment, engineered for success, and endowed with the seeds of greatness."

"What about a man who wasn't endowed with any arms?"

"We're talking about your *potential* now. In your hands you hold the *potential* for greatness."

"I don't *have* any hands."

"What's that? Are you a SNIOP? Do you know what a SNIOP is? A SNIOP is Susceptible to the Negative Influence of Other People. If you're a SNIOP, you'll never become what you want to be."

"I want to be a person with arms."

"One thing you can be sure of: If you don't start, it's a certainty that you can't arrive."

"Are you telling me I *can* have arms?"

"No one on the face of this earth can make you feel inferior without your permission."

"I only feel inferior to people who have arms. If we could lick that one, I wouldn't feel inferior anymore."

"One reason many people never attempt new things is their fear of failure."

"Okay, then, I'm going to try it. I'm going to have arms."

"Go as far as you can see . . ."

"I can see myself with arms."

"And when you get there, you will always be able to see farther."

"You're *right*. Now I can see myself with three, four, five arms."

"Your *attitude* is more important than your *aptitude*. We acquire the characteristics of the people we associate with."

"I'm *never* going near another armless person the rest of my life."

"You are the sum total of what goes into your mind."

"I know that now. I've never had arms on my body because I've never put any arms into my mind. Or hands. Or knuckles. Wrists. *Fingers!*"

"You know what an optimist is? An optimist is a person who, when he wears out his shoes, just figures he's back on his feet."

"I, too, am an optimist. When I've worn out my new arms, I'll figure I'm back on my shoulders."

"Set your gyroscope for success!"

"I will."

"Our yearning power is more important than our earning power!"

"I know it."

"Achieving is contagious!"

"I've caught the disease."

"Today is the first day of the rest of your life!"

"I know it, Zig, and I want you to share the first one

with me. Let's *believe* in ourselves today. Let's have a victory dinner."

"Now you're talking."

"I'll drive."

"Sorry, but I have to make a speech this evening. It's called 'Don't Let Failure Make You a Coward.'"

RAMSES, THE ORIGINAL PARTY ANIMAL

Everybody in Dallas spent the better part of a year running over to the Texas State Fairgrounds to see the Big Hoo-Haw Ramses the Great Egyptian Freak Show, trying to figure out why there's so many giant sacred frowning baboons climbing on people's heads. Fortunately, they passed out Sony Walkmans when you went in, and so Charlton Heston told you exactly why the baboons are frowning, whose head they're climbing on, and what kind of great spiritual honor it is to have a baboon perched on your noggin.

What I can't believe is that Charlton would do this at all. Chuck, listen, you can't lead the Jews out of Egypt and then go back in later and decide to *worship the mummies*. See those thirty-five-foot-high statues of Pharaoh? Don't you remember how John Derek was whipped severely to make him build those suckers? It was an experience that ruined his mind for life and led in later years to an obsession with taking nude pictures of his wives. Charlton, Charlton, Charlton, these are the people that wanted to leave you in a floating picnic basket in the *bulrushes*.

I'm not saying that Ramses the Great wasn't a fascinating guy. For example, he built more temples to himself than Donald Trump. Every time Ramses got the hiccups, he said, "Must be a sign from the gods. Send fifty thousand men to Karnak and build a temple to the god with all the *k*'s and *h*'s in his name. No, not Amenhotep. We already built one to him. The other one. Akhenaten-haten. In fact, put four additional *h*'s and four additional *k*'s in the god's name. I want the longest god ever worshipped. I want a temple to Akkhehnahktehn-khaten-khaten!"

And he would build the mother, too. He didn't care how many people died getting the job done.

Another thing about Ramses—the man loved funerals and coffins and crypts. He built a whole city full of em. Then he built a whole city for himself. Then he built a whole city for himself when he was dead. Then he built a whole city for his harem. (The man had ninety children. That we know of.) Then he built a city for his wife. Then his wife died, and so he built a *funeral* city for his wife. The man was a workaholic.

Ramses was one of those guys who liked to marry his sisters and daughters. It's funny how some guys do that and end up doing twenty-to-forty in the Texas State Department of Corrections, and some guys do it and end up owning gold necklaces that weigh fifty-five pounds each.

The Ramses army kicked hiney all over Syria.

Ramses also had a thing for his mother.

Ramses used to run four times around the track to show the Egyptians how immortal he was.

After he couldn't run four times around the track anymore, he declared himself a god and had a special ceremony to install himself in heaven.

One time Ramses had a statue built with two people on it. The first one is Ramses making offerings to a god. The second one is the god, Ramses, accepting the offering from himself.

The number of subjects Ramses ruled over was about the same as the population of Dallas and Fort Worth.

As soon as he became king, he started building his funeral temple, the Ramesseum. It had a statue of Ramses in it that weighed a thousand tons. He was in his nineties when he died, and he still had guys working on it.

When he died in 1213 B.C., it took all the sacred hoo-haw priests seventy days to turn him into a kingly mummy and get him ready for eternal life.

All the stuff they took out of his body was put in jars and buried with him.

There was enough gold on his coffin to pay the national debt of Brazil.

They sewed his heart back in his chest with golden thread.

It took three or four weeks for his sacred mummified body to travel by barge and oxen sled to the tomb. All that time, he was surrounded by dancers, priests, and masked actors. It was all making him immortal, as he passed into the underworld, fought off all the demons in his way, appeased the other gods, learned how to survive in immortality, and took his place in the heavens. All the people of Egypt tried to get close to the body, crying and tearing their hair as he passed. And then three priests finally slid his coffin into the richest tomb ever built, a place built to last a million years, a place blessed by the sun god Ra.

A hundred years later, some burglars sneaked into the Ramesseum and stole all his coffins, lifted all the jewels off his body, ran off with the gold, and took everything else they could get their hands on. All that was left was the mummy. You can see it today if you go to the Cairo Museum. He's perfectly preserved in immortality: short, bald, with abscessed teeth, stooped over from arthritis.

By all means, let's worship him again.

THE GOD OF NEWSWEEK

Newsweek has been taking polls about God again. I hope He's getting sick of it, cause you know what? If seventy-seven people tell a *Newsweek* pollster they believe there's a heaven, and twenty-three people say they don't, God's just liable to say, "Okay, you guys that are so cocksure, there is one can go *right now.*"

Unfortunately, the Big Guy's not as mean as I am, and so He didn't do that.

Newsweek also found out that 76 percent of Americans think they're going to heaven, and only 6 percent are going to hell. It's a good thing my West Texas Babtist pastor, the Reverend T. Bailey Withers, wasn't around to see that, cause he would of been up in the pulpit telling you people that it's only the 6 *percent* that have any chance at all. "Cause there's nothing more dangerous," Reverend Withers would say, "than a man that don't know how much evil is in him."

I've got a better way of figuring out who oughta go to heaven and whether God's getting the place ready for you. The next time *Newsweek* sets up a poll, they oughta ask it like this:

    1. *Have you done everything you can do throughout your entire life to get into heaven?*

Yes: 2 percent. (These people go straight to hell for lying.)

No: 98 percent. (These people still have a chance.)

    2. *Have you done everything you can do* most of the time *to get into heaven?*

Yes: 45 percent. (You ferret out a lot more liars when you ask the question in a vague way. See, they're not really lying to you, they're lying to themselves. Straight to hell.)

No: 55 percent. (These people are still hanging in there?)

    3. *Do you love your neighbor?*

Yes, I believe I do: 65 percent. (Straight to hell for lying.)

No: 2 percent. (Straight to hell for not caring.)

Sometimes: 33 percent. (Okay, we'll ask it in another way.)

    4. *Do you love your neighbor as yourself? Meaning, just as much as yourself?*

Yes: 40 percent. (This is even worse. Get those other guys out of the line. You people go to hell *first*.)

No: 60 percent. (You've got a chance.)

    5. *Do you love your enemy?*

Yes: 5 percent. (Liar, liar, pants on fire.)

No: 5 percent. (Okay, maybe.)

I know He said that, but I don't think that's what he meant: 70 percent. (Absolutely hopeless.)

My enemy? My *enemy!* No way, José! Are you kidding?: 20 percent. (Buy an asbestos suit.)

6. *Do you love that one particular enemy? You know the one? The one that screwed up your whole life? The one that made you lose everything you deserved?*

Yes: 1 percent. (Liar.)

Yes, I forgive him. He was not a nice individual, but I forgive him: 89 percent. (Straight to hell for being a self-righteous jerk.)

Nope: 10 percent. (Still hope here.)

Are you getting the message so far? You see how honesty helps?

And then, if the Reverend T. Bailey Withers was running the *Newsweek* poll, he would ask the question . . .

7. *Based on your life so far, which one do you deserve, heaven or hell?*

Heaven: 20 percent. (There are some schoolmarm types you just can't get through to, no matter what.)

Hell: 80 percent. (Most people know enough theology to answer this one right.)

8. *Based on your future life, now that you know what's going on, which one do you deserve, heaven or hell?*

Heaven: 99 percent. (This one always gets em. Something about the weird stuff you *haven't done yet* that won't quite register in your brain.)

Hell: 1 percent.

"Hallelujah!" the reverend would say to that 1 percent. "You've got what God needs."

Unfortunately, the Reverend Withers and the others like him aren't around anymore, and so people don't know this. Instead, they think "being nice" and "heaven" are the same thing. Or, 94 percent of em do anyway. The rest of em are at a tent revival in West Texas where sinners are forced to read *Newsweek* magazine.

JEW OR NOT JEW?

The parliament over in Israel is debating a new law called "Who is a Jew?" because too many namby-pamby wimp Jews have been getting into the country without memorizing all the books of the Bible in Hebrew and growing proper Moses beards like God intended. But if the real religious political parties win, then the definition of a Jew is gonna get *extremely* serious—chainsaw circumcisions, that sort of thing—and there could be drastic consequences for American Jews. Jackie Mason might never be able to return to his homeland.

Actually, I'm in favor of some stricter definitions of Jewishness. Almost everybody I sent Christmas cards to last year turned out to be Jewish. All my bosses are Jewish. My agent is Jewish. My lawyer is Jewish. I have a Jewish business partner. My accountant is not Jewish, but I'm thinking of firing him for that reason alone. In other words, they're obviously making it *too easy*.

Twenty years ago, a good Babtist growing up in Texas would meet maybe two, three Jews in his life. One was Stanley Marcus, who was always hanging around Neiman-Marcus trying to get you to buy an autographed copy of *Minding the Store*. (In fact, rare-book dealers now charge a thousand dollars a copy for *unautographed* copies of *Minding the Store*.) The other one was the guy who sold you your wedding ring. And then occasionally some Babtist preacher would convince you to go to some meeting where they planned how to "convert the Jews" and convince them in the depths of their hearts that they were the scum of the earth but Jesus loved em anyhow. As far as I know, this never worked on a single Jew, but every year some Holy Roller would try it anyhow.

I don't even care about that stuff anymore. What I'm talking about is beefing up the Jewishness standard, make it tougher to *claim* to be a Jew, unless you can present the proper ID.

For example:

"You're telling me you want to produce game shows? I'm sorry, I just *don't* believe you're Jewish enough. Quick now, which is bigger, Nineveh or Tyre? Do the sages say that King David is holier than King Solomon, or the reverse?"

If the guy can't answer the question, he has absolutely no business working in the garment district.

Or let's say a young would-be Jew wants to go into his father's novelty-fake-nose-and-glasses manufacturing concern. How do you know he's *serious* enough? He's gonna make all this money, maybe go over to Tel Aviv masquerading as a defender of Israel, and we want to know up-front whether he *deserves* it.

Here's what we do. We ask him the following question:

"How many angels could dance on the head of a pin, if the pin is made with strong, sturdy recycled-refuse materials?"

If the guy gives some answer like "more than a thousand"—or if he names *any* specific number—then he's out. Fake Jew. No bar mitzvah.

If he says, "I don't know" or "That's a dumb question," then he's an idiot gentile that slipped into the gene pool somehow. Check with Grandma to see who she messed around with.

But if he answers like this . . .

"How many angels could dance on the head of a pin? There are many answers, my friend. Rabbi Hillel, may God praise his wisdom, would say an infinite number, for God is infinite in his infiniteness. Rabbi Joshua, of the sages of Eastern Shtetl, would say only one angel, for God would see the one angel in particular, and provide for him, and not for the many. But Rabbi Shlemo, of Camden, New Jersey, would say the answer is none, for the refuse business has gone to hell these days and to create the pin would put God out of business. We must mind the scribes and the sages and the oracles of God, for they are many."

This man is a Jew! Please give him an insurance company, a multipicture production deal at Paramount, a newspaper in Arkansas, and an Israeli Platinum Card.

"Who is a Jew?" this man would ask. "We will ask God when we meet Him. Until then, we will keep our mouths shut."

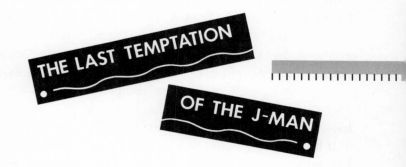

THE LAST TEMPTATION OF THE J-MAN

The problem with movies about Jesus is that you already know how they come out. And that's why *The Last Temptation of Christ* is so great. You never know what this wacky Jesus is gonna do next!

Okay, okay, okay, most of you know by now that I haven't been inside a hard-top movie theater since 1967, and that was only to get change for a twenty. I only watch movies at the drive-in. But I had to see this one. All my Baptist buddies, all my Pentecostal buddies, all my friends in the Citizens for Decency of Tupelo, Mississippi, the ones that had the march on the World Headquarters of 7-Eleven three or four years back—*everybody* was in town for the grand opening. They decided to suggest that the makers of this movie should have their heads blown off in a Christian manner, and they were carrying signs that said stuff like MY SAVIOR THINKS THIS MOVIE HAS COOTIES and other Christian sentiments, and whenever there's a protest of that size, it normally means you're gonna see at least sixty, seventy nekkid breasts and somebody's head exploded. I've been using their recommendations for years.

So all right, yes, I admit it, I'm not proud of it, but I went *indoors* to see this flick. But I know the J-Man will forgive me for that, because this is his best performance in several centuries.

It starts out with Jesus on a bad acid trip. He roots around in the dirt all the time and hangs out with talking snakes and faints and twitches a lot and watches Mary Magdalene make the sign of the triple-jointed electric eel in a cave full of Iranians. Mary Mag has some body tattoos that make her look like she spent the seventies in a biker gang, and she tries to manipulate the J-Man into marrying her by saying she wouldn't have to be imitating the burrowing-back weasel if it wasn't for the fact that Jesus is not into marriage. "Get a life!" she tells him.

One thing I like about this Jesus, compared to the eleven-hour miniseries Jesus, is that this guy doesn't mess around. He does the Sermon on the Mount in, like, two minutes. It's more like the Sermonette on the Mount, and then he gets back to the important stuff, like washing a hooker's feet.

Then, when he finally meets John the Baptist, John looks like he just crawled up out of a Goodwill box. He's a crazy old coot who's been hanging around the Salvation Army office growing stuff in his hair. In fact, it's André! Remember the guy from *My Dinner with André*? It's him! *Nobody* will listen to the guy, and who can blame em? We had to listen to him for two hours already in the other movie.

Anyhow, Jesus makes it out into the desert, sits in the dirt some more, and Satan sends some zoo animals to tempt him. The desert is *always* the best place to be tempted by the devil, which is why I personally spend so much time in Tucumcari, New Mexico. But anyhow, first a snake asks him to look at the snake's garbonzas, but a snake doesn't have garbonzas, so that doesn't work. Then a lion tells him he's a liar. Then a ball of fire talks with a British accent. Jesus eats a big old bloody apple, chops down a tree, and then he goes to see Mary and Martha, who are telling him, "God doesn't want you to fast and pray. He wants you to make children!" As you can see, *now* God's sending the *real* test—*more* women trying to manipulate him into marryin em.

Next thing, Jesus gets some disciples that all look like they oughta be named Akbar, and then he rips his heart out of his chest and shows it to the disciples, and they are *very* impressed. Then he becomes *real* popular with the disciples by turning water into wine, and then he tells his mother to buzz off—we're staying pretty close to Scripture at this point—and then we get to one of my personal favorite scenes: Lazarus. You know, it's not something you like to think about, but when Jesus did that, Lazarus had already been down in that tomb for a couple, three days, and he was *stinky*, besides which he looked like Jason after he's been killed in *Friday the 13th, Part 5*. Then Saul of Tarsus comes along—it's Harry Dean Stanton, the Repo Man!— and he says, "So, Lazarus, how do you feel?" Which is pretty much getting right to the point. And then he asks Lazarus which was better, alive or dead, and Lazarus says, "There wasn't that much difference," and so Saul kills him.

And then the rest of it is pretty much straight out of the Bible until you get to the part at the end where he's nekkid on the cross, trying to figure out *some other way* for the story to end. And then Martin Scorsese, the director, shows us *some other way* for it to end. And that's the part that my buddy Donny Wildmon of the Citizens for Decency says ought to be censored off the face of the earth. It's where this guardian angel that looks like a Valley Girl Brat Pack reject with a British accent comes and gets him off the cross and takes him on a picnic and reintroduces him to Mary Magdalene and they get married, and then she dies, and then he marries the *other* Mary, of Mary-and-Martha fame, only he gets a little from Martha on the side, and then there's a whole lot of that obnoxious Middle Eastern flute music, until he's an old man dying on his bed and he thinks to himself, "You know, I think I did something wrong here," and then Paul and Judas show him that little Brat Packer was really the devil and he better get his hiney back up on the cross where he belongs. And so he does. And it *is* where he belongs. And it *is* a temptation he had. And it *is* something you'd think about if *you* were up there, no matter what my Babtist brothers have been saying.

See, the J-Man's only problem was, when he got up there on the cross, he thought maybe he needed some *help* from his fellow Christians. But they turned out to be no help at all. And it turned out the J-Man didn't need help from people like that anyhow. And nothing's changed a bit.

PART 3

THIS GREAT SICK COUNTRY WE LIVE IN

L ast year I was tooling through Dee Cee trying to sell a book I wrote that has a picture inside it of Bo Derek riding nekkid on a horse, but unfortunately I got to town one day when thirty-seven other guys were taking all the talk-show time with books about how stuff is going to hell. There was a book about how the international monetary system is going to hell, and one about South Africa—I can't remember whether South Africa was going to hell or *investments* in South Africa were going to hell—and one about the CIA, which actually now that I think about it is *always* going to hell. But the bottom line is it was the first city I ever rode into where all these books that I call "hiney-in-a-crack" books—cause they all start out, "Boy, is our hiney in a crack *now!* Whew, are we in *big* trouble!"—like I say, it's the first place I ever saw where these books didn't go straight to the fifty-cent table at Wal-Mart where somebody wearing thongs could buy em all up and truck em over to the old-folks home for charity. Anyhow, I did do this one radio show run by a gal named Diane Rehm, and right before me there were two guys from the Canada Parliament talking about something going to hell in Montreal, and right after me was Arthur Schlesinger, Jr., talking about everything going to hell and, come to think of it, he didn't look too good himself. And I was right smack-dab in the middle, scaring Diane Rehm half to death so that she kept her hand right there on the "black hole" radio censorship button to keep me from talking about Mamie Van Doren's bust line, and about all I had to say was it's a sorry state this country's come to when nobody has time to talk about Bo Derek riding nekkid on a horse. So what I'm getting to here—and I realize that I haven't made my point yet, but this is a book, which is the last place in America where *we don't care how long it takes*—what I'm getting to is, it was my first direct experience with the all-powerful Newnited States Electronic New Age Media. Hiney-in-a-crackers.

Couple days after this experience, I ran into a guy named Jack Limpert, the high sheriff of *The Washingtonian* magazine, and I told him this story that I'm telling you, and Jack asked me to volunteer to study the situation. His plan was that I would go to a remote missile silo in western Kansas, where my brain was wired up for research and I was strapped into a La-Z-Boy recliner and forced to watch the following four tee-vee programs: *Washington Week in Review, Inside Washington, This Week with David Brinkley,* and *The McLaughlin Group.* I did it. I survived. I'm here to talk about it. And let me say, I've seen more than eight thousand exploitation movies in my lifetime, and beyond any doubt whatsoever, these four programs are some of the finest horror shows ever produced. Don't get me wrong. I love ever one of em. After I started watching em, one after another, hour after hour, like being on a freeway full of constant traffic wrecks, the kind of place you can't stand to stay at and you can't stand to leave, I got to where I couldn't even go to the bathroom anymore without finding out what Jack Kilpatrick thought about it. But you know how some people get addicted to drugs, some get hooked on alcohol, some can't beat that craving for chocolate? I'm not real proud about admitting this, but I got hooked on bullshit.

Show you what I mean. Let's start off with the granddaddy of em all, the one that started this whole era of zombie talk shows, *Washington Week in Review,* also known as

BRUNCH WITH THE LIVING DEAD

It might surprise many of you to find out that this show scored a very strong 74 on the Joe Bob Briggs Political-Talk-Show Crock Meter, making it the kind of show you can watch for just three weeks and start to lose all memory of the existence of sexual organs. This is the first sign of a great one, when your eyes, ears, and limbs lose all feeling and your mouth utters the word "caucus" without thinking. When I first started watching these shows, I thought the Iowa caucus was something whores in Des Moines gave you when you didn't have enough money for around-the-world, but, of course, now I know it's something that talk shows give you when you don't have enough money for cable.

Anyhow, let's break this deal down into all the compulsory scores:

The **"Bowling for Dollars" Factor:** These points are awarded for the degree of resemblance between the talk-show set and the set of *Bowling for Dollars. Washington Week in Review* consists of a blue table the size of Montana and a gray wall. Score: a perfect 10.

The **Bad Hair Factor:** It's essential that every guest on a Washington talk show have little or no hair and bad eyesight for that rumpled "Have another scotch" look. Paul Duke, moderator of the show, gets everybody off on the right foot by pushing his receding hairline, white hair, and goggle glasses right into the camera, reading off some headlines, and then giving one of his wonderful segues into the show: "And the latest abortion decision caused an immediate backlash from family-planning groups. And our *own family* of reporters is . . ." Jack Nelson, the *El Lay Times* guy who's always grinnin like he just got a free rib dinner, has a limp thatch creepin up the dome, and so does Charles Corddry, a brown-suited paperweight who looks like the sponsor of the high school science club, and whose job on the show is to remind us that the *Baltimore Sun* exists. Score for this group: a healthy 8.

The **Lobster Dinner Factor:** Closely related to the Bad Hair Factor, but much more accurate, this one is computed by the average number of steak-and-lobster dinners consumed by each member of the panel during the last week. A score of 5, for example, would mean that each panelist had consumed both an eighteen-dollar appetizer and a twenty-eight-dollar main course on five of the past seven evenings. Scores of 10 are theoretically possible, but only for very serious three-hour-lunch men. For verification, look first to the jowls, next to the ruddy "baked potato" complexion, and finally to the protein-laden belly proper. Nelson and Duke both qualify, but the "Gals" don't (see below), so the disappointing score is: 4.

The "Gal" Factor: At least one woman on the panel, to get the point across that "we let girls play." Ideally she should resemble the wicked stepsister Griselda and wear a collar that's wrapped so tight around her neck that her whole head looks like it got forced up through a sink drain. She'll need some padded shoulders and hair that wouldn't move in hurricane-force winds. Young gals, like Ellen Hume of *The Wall Street Journal*, have got problems, due to the last little pieces of femininity that are still threatening their talk-show careers, which may be why she looks like a deer on the first day of season. It's all right, though, cause she covers it up with stuff like "sensible" glasses and blouses that blend in with the furniture. Fortunately for the show, Christine Russell of *The Washington Post* dresses exactly like the witch of Endorf. Score: 9.

Huge Corporate Sponsor Factor: Any decent political talk show has to have a *disguised* sponsor. So, for example, if it's a big chemical company, you run commercials about crippled kids that need chemicals for their therapy, or whatever else you can think up. You never ever *ever* say, "Buy some of these here chemicals." The commercial comes and goes and you think, "What the heck was that anyhow?" It can't even *look* like a commercial. And on *Washington Week in Review*, they don't even call it a commercial. They call it "funding provided by." The funding seems to be provided by a 1991 Ford Sierra on a swivel platform. Score: 7.

So far we've been in the compulsory categories, but now we can get down to the true nitty-gritty:

The Bicker Meter: Very simple—how much do they really *hate* one another? On *Washington Week in Review,* the Bicker Meter scores extremely low. About the only times it registers are when the decisive Jack Nelson looks at the impetuous Christine Russell and says, "This anti-abortion thing, it probably isn't all that popular across the country, is it?" Score: a mere 2.

The Duff Detector: Nobody on a political talk show should ever actually *know* anything. It takes too long to know anything. To know anything, you've got to take long airplane rides, hassle with people that don't want to talk to you, go to the library. And read actual books. Nobody has time for this. That's why you need to quote *The Washington Post* a lot or, better yet, have Haynes Johnson on your show. Haynes Johnson's job is to make sure that whatever twenty-two-year-old reporter just spent three days of his life tracking down troop movements in the jungles of Papua New Guinea can be described like this: "We have reports coming out of the South Pacific that show you're absolutely *wrong,* Ed." The second rule honored by the Duff Detector is: "Always talk about your vast network of unidentified sources." The best thing to talk about is political campaigns, so that Haynes Johnson can go on about "great uncertainty in this area" or "the Reagan era is over," followed by the decisive proof from Howard Fineman of *Newsweek* that it's *not* over because "I just flew back from Iowa, and so . . ." or the equally convincing "I attended one of the actual caucuses on Tuesday," followed by the master, Hedrick Smith of *The New York Times:* "I talked to one high U.S. official this week who said . . ." or "I talked this week with a foreign ambassador who is very closely involved with this and . . ." This is also called the Heart-of-Darkness Principle, so that no matter what you say, a) you got it from somebody important, and b) if it's wrong, then it wasn't you, it was Them. The crown prince is Charles McDowell, who looks like everybody's goofy uncle and edits the *Richmond Times-Dispatch*, who evaluated the Pat Robertson candidacy by quoting "the people that I talked to today that I trust on these matters." Score: a perfect 20.

The Feedlot Factor: This one takes vast political talk-show experience to figure out, but what it basically comes down to is: Does the show have a sacred opinion that *nobody* will violate because it threatens the whole feedlot? The only way to detect it is when they use the word "we." And the only time this show uses it is when they're talking about the United States, the *official* U.S. government, especially compared to countries like Panama where political talk shows are illegal. "*We* chose to support Noriega in our own selfish interests," says Haynes Johnson, like *The Washington Post* has a weekly CIA strategy meeting. Score: a respectable 14.

Now that you understand the rules, let's mosey on down the street to *Inside Washington*, better known as:

OLD FART JUBILEE

This is the first show I know of that starts off with the high school band overture that we were all forced to play at Arkansas Tech Summer Band Camp in Russellville, Arkansas, in the sixties, but that's okay cause it goes right along with the video graphics, which are basically what we learned to do when we signed up for "Editing 102" at the Video Technical Institute in Bossier City, Louisiana. Let's go right to the scoreboard and check this baby out.

"Bowling for Dollars" Factor: Only a 9. They got fancy and put in silhouettes of the Capitol dome.

Bad Hair Factor: Bingo! We're talking Kojak City. Don't even *think* about hair on this show. That's James J. "Rappin Jack" Kilpatrick on the right ("That's not only *historical*, Gordon, it's *hysterical*"), dressed in a Motel 6 throw rug, shining his head in Carl Rowan's eyes. Brother Carl sits in his chair like a Buddha that hasn't stood up in three years, and somewhere in there we've got Strobe Talbott of *Time*, who should be much too young for Old Fart Jubilee, but he's already nekkid upstairs. Gordon Peterson, the barker, is a baby in the Bad Hair department—he's still got thirty, forty strands left—but he brings in Lou Cannon of *The Washington Post* every once in a while so they can stick *his* dome in front of the Capitol dome. A perfect 10.

Lobster Dinner Factor: Watching these well-fed American Express platinum-card holders is like being trapped at the Steak and Ale salad bar for two weeks with fifty aluminum-siding salesmen. We have a decisive oink factor. Another solid 10.

"Gal" Factor: Elizabeth Drew has shoulders bigger than Sylvester Stallone and talks to everybody like a small-town librarian that's been fattened up for seven years on an East German steroid farm. "They've really closed that stature gap. . . ."

"This is true volatility. . . ." Lady Macbeth scores, of course, a 10.

Huge Corporate Sponsor Factor: Not one but three mega-corporations that evidently don't do anything but save bald eagles and father laughing babies. The first one is something called Valic, which has commercials full of handicapped kids and a bunch of that modular horse-pen furniture you can put your fist through. Then IBM explains how something called "fractile geometry" will help us find God. But the highlight of the show is Weyerhaeuser's tribute to Arkansas wildlife, followed by a documentary on how they helped the Nisqualli Indian Tribe of Beaver Creek, Washington, stock beaver ponds with salmon. For the sheer number of pictures of the woods taken from a helicopter: 10.

Bicker Meter: Think of how the oldest person in your family bickers. He doesn't bicker *at* anybody, does he? He bickers into the void. He bickers at whatever jumps into his mind. He bickers *without even needing anybody to hear his bicker.* That's exactly what we've got here. "The Republican race is truly an unedifying matter now," bickers Elizabeth Drew. "I think it's a *sad* thing to abandon these *Contras,* plays right into the hands of the Soviet Union," bickers Rappin Jack. And after somebody says Ed Meese hasn't been found guilty of anything, Carl Rowan bickers, "Well, it's not good for the attorney general to be constantly running before grand juries defending himself." But the best bickers are the ones that don't seem to relate to anything. "I don't like this flip-flop business," says Jack. Score: 8.

Duff Detector: Why did Bush finish third in the Iowa caucus? "It's just disorganization," explains Rappin Jack. "I can't ex-

plain it. I'm just back from New Hampshire, though, and . . ."
Strobe Talbott the yupster quotes Gertrude Stein and talks about
the "existential problem" George Bush has. Elizabeth Drew
says, "Well, *I* have a problem understanding just what a flexible
freeze is"—and so how can anybody in *Iowa* understand it?
King Carl sits back, waits, listens, finally calls for the floor—and
quotes *The Washington Post*. There. Now we know. These guys
didn't make it to Old Fart Jubilee without knowing the basics:
Never *ever* be the *only* person who thinks *anything*. Again,
perfect consistency except for Strobe, who is too young and
hesitant to fulfill his complete blowhard potential: 17.

Feedlot Factor: We used to have a game in elementary school
called "dogpile." It worked like this: At recess, for absolutely
no reason, somebody would yell, "Dogpile on Frankie Sullivan," and within ten seconds fifteen second-graders would be
sitting on top of Frankie Sullivan. Only the mind of an
elementary-school student knows why this *must* be done at
least once a day. And only the mind of Gordon Peterson
knows why occasionally he'll scream, "Dogpile on Panama!"
("*He* doesn't seem like someone we want to be doing business
with," says Rappin Jack. "He's a highly unattractive, if not
loathesome, figure," says Elizabeth. And then, in a feeding
frenzy, everybody starts frothing at the mouth. "There were
tons of these drugs!" screams Jack. "He was flying this money
all over the place! I read the whole indictment!") But that's
nothing compared to the day the entire panel got furious that
Iowa was gonna have an influence on who was the next president. Rowan started it off: "Not representative of this nation!" And then they all did Geronimos off the high board to
land on the back of the *white farmer* out in the *Midwest* that

can't get home delivery of *The Washington Post*. Iowa, for some reason, *threatens the feedlot!* Score: a perfect 20.

May we have the trumpet fanfare now? It's time for *The McLaughlin Group*, also known as:

LIFESTYLES OF THE LEARNING DISABLED

This show is the gravelly-voice, pit-bulldog champeen of the airwaves, the first show that looks like it was put together by alcoholic wrestling promoters. Right away, McLaughlin, the jowly Nixonite himself, starts screaming into the camera like a bullfrog on acid: "In New Hampshire it's clear that the gloves are *off! Pat!*" This is an animal trainer's command for Pat Buchanan to bark out the first two or three words that come to his mind, even if they're "I need to go to the bathroom!" In fact, if Pat Buchanan screamed out, "I need to go to the bathroom!" nobody would ever notice, cause by the time you figure out what he said, three other people have already talked. It's the new talk-show technique called "dyslexic free association."

"Bowling for Dollars" Factor: McLaughlin has put in swivel chairs and carpet to update the set to, oh, about 1964. Score: 7.

Bad Hair Factor: Morton Kondracke of the *New Republic*, the only "kid" ever allowed on the show, has one of those Frankie Avalon hair helmets that looks like the end of a dirty Q-tip. This is balanced on the other extreme by Jack Germond of the *Baltimore Evening Sun*, who's evidently in training to be a Tibetan monk, and Robert Novak of the Chicago *Sun-Times*, who's got white hair, a nose recently broken with a tire tool, and eyesockets so deep that Weyerhaeuser could send a helicopter in there to film commercials. McLaughlin looks like Captain Binghamton in *McHale's Navy*. Score: 6.

Lobster Dinner Factor: The chinless, anorexic David Gergen of *U.S. News & World Report* brings the steak-and-seafood index way down, but his main purpose on the show is to perpetuate the massive international conspiracy that leads people to believe that *U.S. News & World Report* is still actually published. Actually, the last issue was in February of 1948, and they've been sending out the same magazine every week since then. Score: 4.

"Gal" Factor: The grinnin Eleanor Clift of *Newsweek* wears the ultimate talk-show accessory—milk-white stockings. Everything about her is "sensible," and she keeps her mouth shut when the men are screaming. Score: 9.

Huge Corporate Sponsor Factor: This show gets the best one of all—GE. The commercials are so good that all you can remember is it was something about rock stars, welders, ballet dancers, black kids ridin tricycles, satellites in space, bowling teams in Pittsburgh, microwave ovens, old people, babies, cripples, airplane mechanics, Broadway, the Statue of Liberty, dentists, birthday parties, and a Barry Manilow soundalike singin, "We are *threads* in the *ta-pes-treeee!*" A perfect 10.

Bicker Meter: Yelling, finger-pointing, *"Will you let me finish!,"* *"You're libeling a dead man and you should be ashamed of yourself!,"* and my personal favorite—*"I don't care, we're way over, gotta get out, stop it!"* Sometimes the dueling brain-tumor candidates, Novak and McLaughlin, both look like they're gonna spontaneously combust, especially when they're talkin

about something like homos-in-the-army, but it always makes
Morton Kondracke so nervous that he blurts out some weenie
remark that makes Novak yell, "Dogpile on Kondracke!" and
so Novak and McLaughlin never actually start dukin it. If David
Gergen is around, he brings the whole deal to a halt by opening
his mouth and astounding the audience with his uncanny resemblance to the Cat in the Hat. Score: 19.

Duff Detector: Jack Germond once justified an opinion by saying he *actually attended* an Alexander Haig press conference—
as opposed to the other scum on the panel, who merely watched
it on TV. Novak, the first man in history to file a tax return
marked "Occupation: Obnoxious," depends on a network of
unidentified sources so vast that he can never even remember
who *any* of them are. The purest form of the Duff Debate is
frequently seen on this show, when they argue about *what other
people said,* as in, "Bush said Dole was cheating"; "He did
not—Bush said someone in Dole's campaign was cheating";
"He did not—someone in Bush's campaign, without Bush's au-
thorization, said Dole was cheating"; "He did not . . ." Which,
of course, makes us *all* feel like we could be talk-show stars.
Score: 18.

Feedlot Factor: Sacred god Numero Uno: All things in the world,
including election results, have a *reason.* Sacred god Numero
Two-o: The reason is *knowable.* The single-minded pursuit of
these principles means the show always ends in baby talk: "Bye-
Bye!" Score: 10.

But now, finally, we move to the ultimate political talk show,
the talk show so important the guys sit rigid in their chairs like

they're on thrones, the one called *This Week with David Brinkley,* or

SHUT UP, WE WORK FOR ABC

Kind of disappointing, actually, startin off with the fifteen minutes of slick news minicam footage, followed by a "Background Report," followed by a congressman or some other high sheriff being interviewed by Brinkley, Sam Donaldson, and George Will, followed by the only part we give a flip about—the bull session at the end. In other words, this show spends the big bucks to prove that, hey, we all got condos in Bal Harbour, don't screw with us.

"Bowling for Dollars" Factor: If they want to, they can take a whole crew to the Iowa State Capitol, relight it, and take it over as the ABC Studio of the Week. Score: 0.

Bad Hair Factor: Shampooed, layered, and Vidal Sassooned. Brinkley's made a *career* of dork hair. Score: 0.

Lobster Dinner Factor: They all look like they've been attending Geraldo Rivera's "Aerobi-Host" classes. Score: 1.

"Gal" Factor: Basically they don't mess around with women, except when they have a perky token like Cokie Roberts of PBS, who looks and sounds like a Radcliffe coed that's been to too many sociology classes. Score: 0.

Huge Corporate Sponsor Factor: ABC found a company so enormous and mysterious that nobody's ever heard of it—ADM.

Judging by their commercials, they're *for* ethanol, *against* exports, *for* lettuce, *against* "deadly emissions" of carbon monoxide, and strongly in favor of traveling helicopter shots. Then, because ABC is so huge and it wants *all* the huge corporate sponsors, they also have GE crippled kids and ballet dancers, the BMW 57Oil sedan, IC Industries (Japanese food-store equipment, jet landing gears), a DuPont commercial about how they keep you from getting AIDS, Kellogg's high-nutrition cereal, and both Dentu-Creme *and* Dentu-Gel. Truly astounding: 10.

Bicker Meter: Nonexistent. If McLaughlin ever said, "Is this any way to elect a president?" he would scream it so loud that Novak would want to punch him out. Brinkley points an eyebrow at the ceiling and says, "Is this any way to elect a president?" and it has the same effect as if Bugs Bunny said it. "Yes, I think it is, David," says George Will, and the Bicker Meter drips off to empty: 0.

Duff Detector: Doesn't even apply to these people. These aren't *reporters.* They're video lords: 0.

Feedlot Factor: Very simple. Never, *ever,* under any circumstances, allow the guest, *even if he's the president of the United States,* to think it's his show. When Al Gore tries to answer the question too quick, the even, reasonable tones of Sam Donaldson tell him, "Senator, let me ask all four first, and then you may have all the time you need"—and Al's *eyes droop,* like he just farted at Daddy's dinner party. When Paul Simon makes a remark about platforms making no difference as to who won the 1984 race, George Will asks if he's suggesting that the public is "profoundly frivolous" about voting. Simon is so upset by the remark that he stutters and then, two minutes later, is bogged down in stuff like the unemployment rate, "conventional forces," and—the one phrase guaranteed to get the remote-control buttons snapping—Gramm-Rudman. The man's a goner. Get him out of here so we can talk about him. Go to the commercial . . . and he's *gone*. This is probably the ultimate test of a political talk show. Can you *become* the Feedlot? Can you become such a big Feedlot that they beg *you* for an audience? They did it: 20.

Frankly, I'll take *The Diane Rehm Show*. She lets me talk about Bo Derek riding nekkid on a horse.

I have a request to make. The next time I come to your town, for any reason, do *not* take me downtown to where it used to be a slum but now it's Riverplace Courtyard-on-the-Square Plaza. I've already been to Riverplace Courtyard-on-the-Square Plaza. I went to the one in St. Louis and the one in Minneapolis and the one in Memphis and the one in Little Rock and the one in Milwaukee and the one in Atlanta and I already bought all the magnetic silver perpetual-motion satellite paperweight desk ornaments that I'll be needing for the next seventy, eighty years.

It usually starts out like this:

"Joe Bob, if you're not doing anything tonight, we have a

bunch of people that would like to take you down to Riverplace Courtyard-on-the-Square Plaza."

"Sounds great. What is it?"

"Have you ever heard of Ghirardelli Square in San Francisco, or that place in Boston with all the shops?"

"Yeah."

"Well, it's like that."

"Why is it like that?"

"We built it to attract tourists back to downtown."

"Why?"

"Because all the people that live here are afraid to go there anymore."

"Oh."

So we all go down to Riverplace Courtyard-on-the-Square Plaza, and the first thing we do is we ride around in a horse and buggy and look at the For Lease signs in the windows. The buggy driver tells colorful stories about what used to be there before they built Riverplace Courtyard-on-the-Square Plaza Banc Centre.

"This pharmacy you see on the next block," the driver will say, "was once home to the Runnells Brothers drug chain. They sold out in 1944, and the building was vacant for twenty years. In the sixties it was a men's store, then it was empty again until 1983, when the Riverplace Courtyard-on-the-Square Plaza Historic Renovation Commission purchased the property and turned it into a drugstore again."

"Why?"

"It's on the state register of historic structures. The original owners were very famous. They developed a mustard plaster that was used by President Woodrow Wilson. That's what they say anyway."

"Oh."

Next we head over to Zack's Eatery and Bistro for some mozzarella fry-sticks, barbecue blackened shrimp fajitas, and baked lobster gumbo. I can't begin to tell you how happy this makes me.

Now that we're full—"Save room for some of our sinful crepe-on-a-stick later"—we head for a relaxing ride on the *Queen Belle* riverboat and party barge. It's not till we get on board that they tell us a) it doesn't go anywhere except to the next bend in the river, b) there aren't enough plastic deck chairs, c) it takes three hours, and d) there's nothing to do on board except order up some Greek orange sherbet surprise at Ye Olde Ice Creame Shoppe.

Exhausted by so much fun in one day, we don't have much time left for shopping at the multilevel downtown mall, full of stores that sell T-shirts with Kareem Abdul-Jabbar on the front, restaurants that sell cinnamon rolls the size of Montana, and shops called Creations by Erika.

"Joe Bob, there's one more thing we could do."

"Great."

"Did you know that this is one of the best comedy towns in America?"

"Nope."

"We have *eight* comedy clubs. We could go to any of them, but my favorite is Lotta Yuks over on the old wharf."

"Sounds great. Who's there tonight?"

"You're gonna love this guy. Mike Manzonotti. He's been on Letterman twelve times."

"Why?"

"And you know what you're gonna love about him? His sense of humor reminds me of *you*. He's such a wacky guy."

"I'm not a wacky guy."

"See there, you crack me up. You know that joke you do about the dirt-miners in West Texas? Well, Mike Manzonotti does almost the same *exact* joke!"

"Small world, isn't it?"

"So, Joe Bob, have you enjoyed your stay here in the city?"

No.

I hope I've made this clear.

THE LOAN-STAR STATE

Out here on the open range of America, where we shoot the deer with double-barreled shotguns and pump-action elephant rifles and cage up the antelopes and send em down to zoos in Guatemala and keep a few buffalo penned up for tourists and sledgehammer little calves to death for *your* benefit, we got the holy bejabbers beat out of us the last couple years. You probly heard about it.

Oh, sure, you laugh now. You look at us down here, cheated out of all the awl money our granddaddies drilled up out of the ground and piped up to Bloomington, Minnesota, so they could sit around in stupid wool hats and say, "Hey, Olaf, more beer for me!" You laugh, cause you don't know *who puts the food on your table.* And I'm here to tell you who that is.

It's the plain, simple, clean-livin, God-fearin, gum-flossin, tobacco-spittin, fingernail-chewin Texas Realtor.

Lemme show you what I'm talkin about. The following is the complete economic history of Texas:

First the Indians owned it. We killed all of them and sent the leftovers to Oklahoma.

Then the Catholics owned it. We didn't kill any of them, but we should have.

Then the Meskins owned it. We killed most of them and send the leftovers to Mexico, but a lot of em sneaked back in.

Then the people that got kicked out of Tennessee came down and kicked the Catholics out of the Alamo and they got wiped out by a really fat Meskin.

Then the people that got kicked out of ever other state in America came down here and started Houston and started killin one another.

Then the Texas Rangers were invented to make us stop killin one another, except when they weren't looking.

Then we struck awl and got so rich we could hire other people to kill each other.

Then we let some Meskins back in to work at Denny's.

Then we paved it.

Then we killed the president, but it wasn't our fault.

Then we got cable.

Then we all got security alarm systems on our ranch-style brick homes with microwave.

Then—now this is the important part, listen up now—then 7 million dingbats in high heels migrated down here from Chicago so they could wear dangly earrings, wax their bodies twice a month, buy twin-peaked attack bras, and glue on plastic fingernails the size of Chile.

We went crazy. We started givin these women our money. Wouldn't you? Most people, they gotta think back to 1957, 1958, the era of Mamie Van Doren, to find bimbos harnessed up like that.

We started sayin, "Yes, as a matter of fact, I *do* need to trade my crummy little $150,000 house in for a $400,000 restarter home with training pool."

And so pretty soon we were all runnin around like rabid weenie dogs, sayin, "Oh yeah, I live in Twin Dripping Valley Stream Estates. You haven't heard of it? I bought my zero-lot-line modified-Tudor ranch-style with game room on a thirty-year balloon payment three-point floater for just $289,000 in '82, and by '83 the same identical house was sellin for $1.4 million."

And so you'd say, "Well, I just have a little place over in town. It's paid for."

"Paid for? Paid for?" At this point the guy would fall over on his back like a writhing beached sperm whale and make a sound like an NBA team singing "Moon River." It's a very upsetting sound.

"Okay, okay, so how do I get into Twin Dripping Valley Stream Estates?"

"You kidding? You couldn't get in there *now* for a billion dollars. You need to go out north, to Twin Dripping Valley Stream: The Second Edition. Or else you could go out to Possum Kingdom Lake and buy a time-share Dockominium. If you get there on the right day, you can get special deals—free bait for a year, stuff like that. Shop around. If I was you, though, I'd try Lyle Mudbone Shores."

So pretty soon you'd have the car down off blocks, and you'd be putterin out there headed for Lyle Mudbone Shores ("Where the Water's Full of Crappie and the People Are Full of Friendly"). And as soon as you pulled up in front of the Lyle Mudbone Visitors Hospitality Center, *before you even got out of your automobile,* one of these dragon ladies would be out there with her complimentary electric golf cart, ready to go for your groceries. And so for the next two, three hours, it'd just be you, her and Maybelline, tryin to figure out just exactly where you wanted your Dockominium to be on the day when your life changed and you made that big decision to "Walk on Water at Lyle Mudbone."

By the time they got you into the little Assistant Manager's Free-Coffee Room, which had a time lock on the outer door, you'd be pretty much ready to donate your right titty to science if it would get you the title deed three days quicker. So what you do is you basically give this lady the rest of your income for the rest of your life, and do you know why?

Cause it's Texas propty.

And you know what they say about Texas propty?

"It's never lost value in a hunnerd and fifty years, it's only gained."

"They ain't makin any more of it."

And, finally, you got this one: "I sold one of these last year for—Dwayne, what'd we sell that double-wide Swiss Family Robinson Giraffe unit for? Three?—I sold one of these last year for three thousand, and this year, accordin to the latest appraisal we had just last month, it's *already* worth one hunnerd ninety-six thousand dollars unimproved."

And so, pretty soon, you end up with the Captain Ahoy Two-Bedroom Time-Share Getaway Dockominium on Possum King-

dom Lake, and you don't even intend to go there. It's an
investment. Also, you've made a friend for life named Gladys.

So what I'm tryin to tell you is this is what we were doin
down here for about fifteen years, up till a couple years ago. We
were buyin Dockominiums, and party bass boats, and
.0000000003 shares in *Rambo*, and .00000000000001 shares
in awl wells all over the lot, and VCRs and VDTs and satellite
earth dishes that get all the stations in Cuba, and remote-control
doohickeys that make your TV display the Vegas odds on jai
alai, and Eyetalian sports cars that we kept all covered up under
the carport, cause everthing was an *investment*.

That's what Gladys came down here from Chicago with her
skintight panty hose to tell us.

It was an *investment*.

Like in, "Oh no, I don't care nothin about camel-suede suit-
cases with gold latches and secret underwear drawers. I just got
em for an *investment*."

But nobody ever did tell us how maybe, if they started drillin
up too much awl out of the ground over in Abu Dhabi, un-
leaded could go to sixty-four cents and then you know what?

There's a well-known principle of economics, and it goes like
this:

"Any consumer who desires a Dockominium for any other
reason besides living in and using said Dockominium, who then
purchases said Dockominium under bull-market conditions, in-
tending not to realize the full value of his property but to resell
said Dockominium according to a Domino Theory of Perpetual
Unrealized Value, leading to endless vistas of rapidly accumu-
lating profits—such a consumer is, in the final analysis, shit out
of luck."

Of course, Gladys doesn't stick around to tell you this. One day, you just go out on your front porch and pick up the newspaper and the headline says, LYLE MUDBONE INTERNATIONAL FILES FOR CHAPTER 11: DOCKOMINIUM MAGNATE BLAMES UNFAIR JAPANESE COMPETITION, and then you keep readin on down into the fine print at the bottom of the article and you find out that your particular Dockominium unit has been taken over by the Sewage Canal Workers Pension Fund of Amsterdam, Holland, and starting next month you're supposed to send your balloon payment to a man named Lars in Van Nuys, California.

The next thing that happens is the repo man shows up at your door, and he tells you he has to take back your entire set of platinum-plated Mr. Macho Nautilus exercise machines because your collateral on that particular loan has been revalued from $1.9 million to $19.

And then, of course, the word gets around about the repo, and who finds out but Steve Westcott, owner of Westcott La Europeanée Foreign Import and Wreckin Yard, and before you know it—*whammo!*—your wheels are sittin on the courthouse steps, gettin bought up by H. Ross Perot.

By that time the cat's out of the bag. You go on back over to the trailer house that you quit livin in around 1969, and you go hire Bubba Barclay, the famous Dallas bankruptcy lawyer ("Don't Pay, Use Barclay"), and then you spend the next ten years of your life going to depositions.

"Mr. Briggs, in the year 1983, during the month of July, did you affix your signature to a check made out for five thousand dollars and endorsed by Pat's Party Girls of Lawton, Oklahoma?"

"I did."

"And what was the nature of this expense?"

"As I recall, it concerned a soybean-oil contract."

"Were you buying or selling soybean oil?"

"I don't recall."

"Did you, in fact, take delivery on any soybean oil whatsoever during the course of your so-called business career?"

"Yes, I did, but it was for personal consumption."

Sometimes these depositions can go on for *weeks*, and if you use Bubba, then for *months*. Cause as soon as Bubba gets to take *his* depositions, he asks stuff like, "Mr. Briggs, isn't it true that you would be worth at least a hundred million dollars today if the federal government had simply stayed out of your roasted-walnut-Christmas-package-door-to-door-sales business?"

"That is correct. And we wouldn't have near the depression in the walnut industry that we have today."

"Mr. Briggs, have you ever heard the term *pyramid scheme*?"

"Not until the 341 counts of the indictment."

"And you have never participated in such a scheme, have you?"

"My only business was making people rich by sittin around and waitin on other people to sell the walnuts."

"I guess it's a crime in this country to get rich these days, isn't it?"

"Seems like that's what we're coming to, it sure does."

"I have no further questions of this poor man."

But then, of course, the deposition fun only lasts, like I say, five, ten years, and after that's over, you still have got to do something with your Dockominium. I decided that, no matter what else happened, I wanted my little piece of Possum Kingdom to be sold by a woman with really long fake fingernails, even longer than Morgan Fairchild's, and I wanted her to have *two* little electric golf carts, and I wanted her to have enough money for a three-year supply of Mary Kay products, and I wanted . . . but what I wanted was Gladys.

The problem is, Gladys was gone. She'd moved off, her and all 7 million of the other Texas Realtors. I couldn't find em anywhere. They're all living in Phoenix.

H ave you ever been toolin down the interstate in
the middle of the afternoon, punchin radio buttons, and the National Public Communist Radio station comes
on and they're interviewin some fiddle-playin whiskey-voiced
whittler from Sawhorse, West Virginia, who sings a song about
how his mule fell in a sinkhole and twisted his head off? Do you
know the kinda program I'm talking about? For *twenty minutes*
they'll go on and on talking to "the famous storyteller from
Grand Forks, Nebraska—Jessie Wimberly!" And then Jessie will
tell a story about how Mama used to make the greatest buck-
wheat pancakes in Friar Tuck County. And then the announcer
will say, "Our next selection is an early cantata by the minor

German composer, Vilhelm Engel. This is his Opus 134, also called 'Pastoral for the Reich.' "

Have you listened to these shows, or am I the only person? It's like I can't hit the button and change the station. I get transfixed, like watchin a really bad traffic wreck, and I just keep wondering who makes these shows, what dirt bunker in Mexico they've been living in for the last thirty years, and who they think they're sending em out to?

Do they have meetings where they sit around and say, "You know, we have an obligation to the public to produce shows about one-legged religious nuts in Bozeman, Montana, who live in Indian hogans built out of mud and their own spit"? I guess then they send out teams of investigative reporters, fanning out through Montana, to find just the right person who can go on the radio and tell a story about people that hunt beavers with a bow and arrow and make pants out of the skins and say stuff like, "You know, this country used to be beautiful before the developers got here."

But here's one thing I wanna know. When the scratchy-voiced, whiny old lady from East Wendover, Utah, comes on the radio to tell her story about how her Chihuahua got stuck in a car radiator, do they ever ask the people in East Wendover, Utah, what *they* think about her? I wanna know whether the old lady's next-door neighbor wants to hear this story. *Then* I'll decide whether it should be put on National Public Communist Radio.

And what's this connection between 102-year-old centipede collectors in Maine and nineteenth-century opera? What exactly is this market that listens to the radio in the middle of the afternoon and wants to hear about totem-pole carving *and* where Beethoven premiered his Fourth Symphony? Have you ever met a person like this? I have an idea this is not your typical

Miller Lite drinker. How about those guys that wear overcoats in the summertime and sleep in the library all day? They might enjoy this type of programming.

Last summer I was driving through eastern Kentucky and one of these Communist Public Radio shows came on, and it was some guy from rural Pennsylvania telling a story about a cow that some kids hoisted up into a hayloft and how the cow got stuck up there. Now I don't know about your town, but where I live, we've got these old guys that play dominoes all day and ever once in a while they'll go in the coffee shop and tell a story like that, and if they're *lucky,* the dog will be listening. But this deal was goin all over eastern Kentucky.

The only thing I can figure out is the people that put on these shows never have *been* to western Pennsylvania or eastern Kentucky or North Texas or East Wendover, Utah, and so they never have figured out how *boring* most of these people are. It's kinda like when you go to London, and every single person you meet is interesting just because of the way they talk. And that lasts about one day, and then you find out they're even *more* boring than the people back home. So the novelty wears off.

I think that's probly it. These people play a little Beethoven, make themselves feel better, and then they say, "Here's a person I'd probly never even say howdy to if I saw em in the diner, but, come on, it'll be fun to listen to em for five minutes." And then all those people waiting on the Monteverdi Retrospective to come on can think to themselves, "Yeah, boy, that was real America, wasn't it? I'm glad we've got that in America. I'm glad we've got zoos, and I'm glad we've got those people. Very good." And then they put on some more of the "Symphonic Interlude for Tuba and Oboe."

Yeah, I think that's probly what it is.

Things people say to you when you're going on *The Tonight Show:*

"Are you nervous?"

"Will you make a special signal for me?"

"That's a Tuesday. Johnny won't be there."

"Are you making up jokes in advance?"

"Just be yourself."

"I hope you aren't making up jokes in advance."

"You don't seem nervous about it."

"Jay Leno is perfect for you. He'll be much better than Johnny."

"Too bad you couldn't be on with Johnny."

"Here's a joke you can tell. . . ."

"Are you afraid you'll bomb?"

"Usually the comedian gets bumped."

"Your type of humor would be better on Arsenio."

"Even if you're nervous, don't *act* nervous."

"Do that joke about the prairie dogs."

"If you do good with Jay, maybe they'll let you go on with Johnny."

"Your type of humor would be better on Letterman."

"Will Ed be there?"

"Ed will laugh even if no one else does."

"Do you get to meet Doc?"

"Jay does whatever Johnny tells him."

"They might not understand your type of humor on the network, but don't worry about it."

"You seem nervous."

Things people say to you after you've been on *The Tonight Show:*

"What was Jay really like?"

"You didn't seem nervous at all."

"You were nervous at first, weren't you? I could tell."

"I counted the laughs. You had five big laughs and a few little ones."

"Did you make up those jokes in advance?"

"They let you sit on the couch. That's *very* significant."

"Jay really understood your type of humor."

"Jay didn't really understand what you were trying to do, did he?"

"Most of the people couldn't tell how nervous you were."

"Did you get to meet Dennis Hopper? Does he still do a lot of drugs?"

"Why wasn't Ed there?"

"You forgot to make a signal for me."

"Your hair looked really long."

"You made that signal for me, didn't you?"

"This is really the big time for you, Joe Bob."

"Can I have your autograph? It might be worth something someday."

"You were much funnier than Connie Chung."

"Connie Chung was even more nervous than you were."

"Do you think they'll invite you back?"

"It takes at least twenty appearances on *The Tonight Show* before you make it to the big time."

"Maybe Arsenio will want you now."

"Did you meet anybody famous in the greenroom?"

"Maybe next time you won't be so nervous."

I went out to visit the relatives in Waxahachie, Texas, and check on the progress of the new plant that's going in, the Superconducting Supercollider.

The goal of the Superconducting Supercollider is to understand the meaning of time and space in the universe. Physicists are coming to Texas from all over the world to put in their two cents' worth on what's gonna be the most enormous physics experiment ever built.

So now there are two things my family is concerned with: 1) why there's nothing good on TV, and 2) the meaning of time and space in the universe.

"They say they're gonna spend ten billion in town," said my first cousin, Willie Strode. "I haven't seen none of it yet."

151

The reason Willie hasn't seen none of it yet is that Willie never finished his motel-management degree at the community college.

Out on U.S. Highway 287, there's a new business called the Supercollider Auto Body Repair and Salvage Yard.

And the only other evidence of the Superconducting Supercollider is that two years ago everybody was complaining that you couldn't make any money at cotton and you couldn't make any money at alfalfa and you couldn't make any money at cattle, and so you might as well just pack up and move on out to Oklahoma—but this year they're saying, "I don't see how I could part with my farm for less than two thousand bucks an acre."

Suddenly, now that the government needs to build a fifty-four-mile tunnel so that physicists can go down under the ground and study Leptons and Quarks and Neutrinos and intermediate-vector Bosons, this has become "some of the finest blackland farming country in America."

"My daddy farmed this land, and his daddy before him, and his daddy before him," Leotis Scully was telling me. "You can't just up and leave land like this because the university sends some nerds with clipboards out here. That would be taking food out of the mouths of the American consumer."

This is quite a speech for Leotis, since the only thing he normally says is: "The high school football team ain't worth diddly squat this year. They got midgets playing."

So I said to Leotis, "Now how do you figure selling your land to the government is gonna take food out of people's mouths? You don't *raise* food, Leotis. You raise cotton."

"I was thinking of changing to soybeans," Leotis said.

"Oh, that's *different*. That will *definitely* change the government's opinion of you. By all means, they can't have any more of those *soybean shortages* that have been devastating the economy. Then maybe the year after that you can graduate up to *green beans*. That'll *really* make the government think twice. Then you'll be endangering the elementary-school cafeterias all across the country. I can see it on *60 Minutes* now: 'I'm Mike Wallace, and believe it or not, our own government is trying to shut down Leotis Scully's farm, the backbone of our entire food system.'"

Leotis didn't think this was funny.

"It's two thousand an acre," he said to me. "That's what the land is worth."

"All right, Leotis, just how did you *arrive* at that figure?"

And he told me. He explained how, without his land, nobody will ever find out whether the Tau Neutrino exists. And, furthermore, the quark might not even be the basic building block of matter; we might need to go down to the ingredients inside the quarks, or "preons." And think how much better place this world would be if we could be sure that preons exist and the universe is constructed of preons.

"Leotis, you been reading *Time* magazine again?"

He didn't answer me right off.

"What we're doing out here, Joe Bob, is we're reconstructing the Big Bang that happened at the birth of the universe. It's like a cross between the Bible and *Star Wars*."

"Leotis, I've never heard you talk about the process of *anything* being created except the time you took the tour through the Jack Daniel's distillery in Tennessee and found out they make charcoal briquets out of the leftover wood."

"Joe Bob, if this thing works, Waxahachie could be the place where they find out where God lives."

"Are you crazy, Leotis?"

"You've got your New Age influences. You've got your high-energy physics. You've got your Muon Neutrinos. . . ."

"Is this gonna go on much longer?"

". . . You've got your Gluons and your intermediate-vector Bosons. You've maybe got your supersymmetric particles. . . ."

"But what is all that stuff really worth, Leotis?"

"That's what I'm getting at, Joe Bob," he told me. "It's worth two thousand bucks an acre."

What if a white man—let's say a professor of anthropology at Kansas State University—discovered an Indian culture in Utica, Michigan, that had *never been studied*? Let's say the name of this tribe was the Helioscrotum Indians, and there had never been a book about the Helioscrotums. There had never been a study of their body-painting rituals. They'd never received any government grants from the Bureau of Indian Affairs. They'd never even had a single tourist come to visit. They were such boring Indians that they all drove Chevy Caprices and ate at Burger King.

What if—of course, I'm into pure fantasy here, this could never happen—but what if the professor of anthropology at

Kansas State did *nothing*? What if he let all the Helioscrotums die off one by one, or move away, or stop speaking in the rare Helioscrotum dialect of *Ojibwa Winnebago*? What if most of the younger Helioscrotums married Jews, and so after a while we didn't know *what* they were?

Wouldn't it be nice?

Wouldn't it be nice if we didn't have to listen to the guy in Kansas go on for the rest of his life about how the Helioscrotums invented the ancient game of "pierce-the-rabbit-with-a-sharp-stick"? Wouldn't it be nice if he didn't present any academic papers on how the Helioscrotum ritual of eating peyote beans out of a rubber gourd is similar to the Apache firewater mating dance? Wouldn't it be nice, for one time in the history of civilization, if an Indian leader said, "My heritage? No, can't say I remember what those guys five hundred years ago did. I've been in psychotherapy for seven years trying to *forget* my heritage." Or if, perhaps, some of the junior-high-age Indians could grow up going to Van Halen concerts without feeling guilty that they aren't home learning the Dance of the Dying Brave.

I know what I'm talking about. I *was* the Dying Brave. For three years running in the late sixties, I was on the national "Order of the Arrow" Indian-dance champeenship team. There were twelve of us white boys, Super Scouts, who painted ourselves brown and learned every Plains Indian ritual ever practiced. We sewed our own leather breechcloths, beaded our own rib-plates, rehearsed intricate dance steps, and, several times a year, scared the bejabbers out of our parents, relatives, friends, and anyone else who came to one of our ceremonies at the "secret" dance grounds in a rural part of Arkansas. We became so fanatical about this that we actually *performed* the Apache fire dance, which involved leaping *through* a line of flaming torches that stood about four feet off the ground. We did a snake dance with live snakes in our mouths. (For those who wondered how it was done, I can now reveal . . . they were harmless hog snakes, frozen for twelve hours prior to the ceremony, so they squirmed like crazy, but they were not really conscious. We placed rubber masking tape around the part of the snake actually held in the mouth.) For eighteen months I practiced the Tomahawk Dance, which involved flipping a sharp tomahawk into the air repeatedly while dancing at top speed, and then, for the finale, hurling it about thirty feet into the air and catching it.

In other words, we, like the Kansas State professor, were fanatics. We used to talk about exactly *why* we were fanatics. Was it because we'd repeated the rituals so many times that we were starting to *believe* in the Great Spirit, or the Spirits of the Four Winds, or He Who Resides in the Mount? Sometimes, when we would chant the old songs of the Quapaw Indians, the adults in the crowd would actually cry. (Of course, some of them were crying because they'd finally discovered something their sons could do, no matter how weird it was.) We began to think there was a power in the dances, and the songs, and the costumes, and, especially, the silence. For before we began, the dance leader would always slap the main drum violently and command, "Silence!" And, for some odd reason, these middle-class Anglo-Americans, who were rarely ever silent at any time in their lives, would grow very still. And we would let the stillness continue for perhaps five minutes—too long, an uncomfortably long time for people to be still. And then we would charge out of the darkness, torches blazing, sail through a bonfire, four of us, in a crossing pattern, showering sparks onto the dirt, and they would sit in silence through the rest of the rituals. It was the silence that got em, we always thought. It was the silence that convinced them they were in the presence of something supernatural.

But, of course, it was nothing of the sort. It wasn't the Great Spirit, or Wakan Tanka, or Great Manitu, or He Who Makes the Wind. It was a joint manipulation. We were manipulating them, and they wanted to be manipulated. We all wanted to believe that in some other time, some time before we existed, there was a god more important, more powerful, than the lame ones we have today. And we wanted to believe, too, that the Indians had something that we don't have, and that, if we tried hard enough to re-create the outer trappings, we could tap into that power. We could get some of that soul. We could feel a peace that eludes us in other places.

Of course, this was pure bull. Those Indians were no different from us. They had the same doubts. They had the same hopes. They had the same fear. When they did these dances and rituals, they were manipulating themselves into feeling better for a time. So, when we did the dances all those many years later, it made *us* feel better for a time. It's not too hard to understand.

But it's not something we should be preserving. It's something we should be setting aside. It's over. The rituals are done. Wakan Tanka is dead.

This Thanksgiving, let's all agree, the Anglos and the Indians, that we don't need to know why the Indians are here, or where they came from, or which of their rituals should be saved. They're here. That's enough. They don't have to be Indians anymore if they don't want to. They can be Americans. We're the same now.

My friend Chuckie Cadwallader lives in El Lay, and he's like most people in El Lay, he likes to talk, and recently he was telling me about This Great Country of Ours.

Chuckie's traveled all over This Great Country of Ours. All the states. All the states that Make This Country Great. Chicago, Atlanta. All the states. Actually, though, Chuckie doesn't travel much to Chicago or Atlanta anymore—or what was that other one he used to go to all the time? Denver. He doesn't travel much to Denver anymore. He travels mostly between New York and California.

Of course, there's a lot of New York City Chuckie's never

really looked at. Staten Island, nobody ever goes over there. The Bronx, Brooklyn, Queens—Chuckie knows a little about Queens because of the airport. Great airport in Queens. No, what Chuckie's really talking about, the place where you got your real America, is Manhattan. The island. The Big Apple.

Not that Chuckie's seen much of the island. Harlem he only saw the one time, when they went up there to shoot a commercial in an old studio. The limo didn't wanna pick him up at night—boy, was *that* an experience! Greenwich Village, that's a great part of New York, Chuckie used to go down there to see weird plays and movies. Of course, that was ten or fifteen years ago, when Chuckie went to a lot of plays and movies. Now Chuckie mostly goes to midtown and the skyscraper canyons. Not Forty-second Street, though, and not Times Square. No sir. Chuckie remembers when Forty-second Street was Forty-second Street. He would never go near there now. But the rest of midtown—about Forty-eighth to Fifty-seventh, between Park Avenue and Sixth. Donald Trump's neighborhood. Now *there's* your Manhattan, there's your New York, there's your America. You gotta show your face around midtown. There have been times when Chuckie traveled to midtown twelve, fifteen times a year.

This year, though, Chuckie's only been there once, and he didn't like it very much. It was kind of dull. When you think about it, Chuckie says, midtown is not your power center like it once was. Chuckie doesn't really need to travel to midtown as much as he once did. No, a lot of your power centers have gone on out to California, so California is what Chuckie really knows about. That's where he *really* gets around.

Of course, the capital of California is Sacramento, but Chuckie's never been there. He always thought he would need to go there, but he doesn't really. He's heard it's nice, though. San Francisco—now *there's* a great town, even though Chuckie doesn't go there anymore either. All the banks moved their biz to Southern California. San Francisco's great for weekends, tourist stuff, but Chuckie doesn't have much time for that right now. And all the rest of California is not much to speak of in the way of your power centers. It's about like Oregon, or Arizona, or another one of those states like Nebraska.

No, *Southern* California is where it's happening, where you've got your real power centers. That's where you need to know your stuff. That's the part of America that Chuckie knows like the back of his hand. Well, except for the obvious parts, like Watts, where he never has managed to visit, or San Bernardino, which he never does have any reason to go to. San Diego's great—what a zoo! Chuckie used to go to Hollywood a lot, but it's dirty now, it's not what it used to be. Downtown El Lay is really *booming,* isn't it, Chuckie's gotta get down there one of these days and have some Japanese food. Every once in a while Chuckie talks to the secretaries around the office about what it's like out in Glendale and Anaheim and Oxnard and Costa Mesa, and someday Chuckie would like to drive out and take a look at those places. Chuckie used to go to Pasadena every year for the bowl game, but he doesn't have much energy for that anymore.

No, when you think about it, Chuckie's seen every bit of This Great Country of Ours, he knows all about it, and, you know, you don't even have to go much farther than down-town Beverly Hills. That's what you call your power center. That's your America.

NEW YAWK AND DEE CEE

(Written for the "Washington vs. New York" issue of *Newsweek*)

Making a comparison between New York City and Dee Cee is like asking who has the best disco in Guatemala. There might be a moment in your life when you'll need the information, but only if you're already such a brain-damaged zombie-face mush-head that you went to Central America looking for a party.

Everybody that moves to New York goes there for the same reason: "Well, you know, we had to, for my career. My heart will always be in Duluth, but really, New York's not such a bad place. There are so many *cultural opportunities*." Now, for the first time anywhere, the *Joe Bob Briggs Guide to the Cultural Opportunities of New York and Dee Cee.*

Housing: There haven't been any houses in New York since 1674. So everyone now lives in rent-controlled Kleenex boxes. People in New York love to tell you about their particular personal Kleenex box. Some of em live by Central Park in Kleenex boxes with bay windows. Others live in Greenwich Village in Kleenex boxes that used to be perfectly decent industrial power-tool storage closets. You can buy a high-rise Kleenex box, if you want one, for about the same money it would take to buy Brazil. In Dee Cee, people don't live in Kleenex boxes. They live in Maryland. Except for the rich people, who live in Virginia, except for the really, really rich people, who live in Dee Cee next door to the ambassador from Esmeralda, except for the poor people, who live in Dee Cee in Kleenex boxes. Which brings us to:

Commuting: Every New Yorker is the *only* guy who has figured out the secret to commuting, but he's willing to share the secret with you—as in, "Actually, we live in a small town in Indiana, but it's an *easier commute* into Manhattan than if we lived on Thirty-fourth Street." In Dee Cee, people will tell you about something called a Beltway. The only way to make them stop doing this is to gently but firmly plant your foot between their eyes. But the commute is worth it because of:

Night Life: Let's start with Dee Cee, whose idea of night life is the Kennedy Center, which has shows starring Lebanese boys choirs that you'd be better off watching on PBS, where you don't have to wear a tuxedo. In New York, Lincoln Center serves the same purpose, but the difference is that Dee Cee can only afford shows like Tibetan acrobats that dance on their elbows. In New York, you can see some *real* culture, like lesbian ballet companies that dance old *I Love Lucy* episodes while chanting "Death! Death! Mother! Mother! Pizza! Pizza!"

"But we have *the Theater* here." Yeah. Right. So why is it that nobody who lives in New York can ever tell you what's playing, who's in it, or what it's about? Because nobody in New York has *attended* the theater since 1928. *We* are the ignorami—the people out here in the boonies—who go to the Broadway shows. We do it every year when we take Grandma on vacation so she can see Betty Buckley screaming at the top of her lungs, or, if we really wanna get our hundred dollars' worth, Mary Tyler Moore as a paraplegic.

In Dee Cee, they have museums and monuments that nobody who *lives* in Dee Cee ever goes to—they watch cable like all of us—but the museums and monuments only make us hate the place even more. The Smithsonian Institution is such a great set of museums it reminds us what interesting politicians we *used* to have, instead of the third-rate lawyers and Go Kart–track owners we've got now.

Business: *Now* I get it. Who could resist these two cities when you see what centers of the universe they are? What young, ambitious attorney could pass up the opportunity to be a junior partner in a Wall Street firm that advises Canadian liquor conglomerates on the strategies for suing Scottish competitors in American courts to leverage hostile takeover attempts against Caribbean holding companies that build condos in Tokyo? What city besides New York could find a role model in Donald Trump, who achieved the American Dream by charging megabuck rents on the Kleenex boxes, then reinvesting the money in New Jersey gambling operations, and putting his name on more stuff than Vanderbilt ever did? In Mississippi, they'd call that "white trash."

But Dee Cee is the place where the American dream is *really* alive. That's the city where you can start out sorting mail for an undersecretary of agriculture, jump over to the Internal Revenue Service to be the head of misleading consumer information, move to Bethesda, get a transfer to Congress as the aide of your hometown representative, wait until he exposes himself in a public park, write a book about it, and end up with your own show on CNN. Nobody wants to be president anymore. The role model here is Al Neuharth, the man who exemplifies the aspirations of the media today: He brought the color weather map to every household in America.

One time I took this special train called the Metroliner that both New York and Dee Cee are real proud of because it makes the run between the two downtowns in three hours. Actually, it's like being on a Wild Mouse for three hours, bucking up and down and side to side, jostling your complimentary Styrofoam cup all over your custom Naugahyde seat cover, while outside you see all these suburbs and industrial plants and, every once in a while, somebody just standing there gawking as you race by on your way to Someplace Very Important. This person is still, quiet, unmoving—unlike you. When you see him standing there in what looks like solitude, you get the sensation of being on a nightmarish ride from one part of hell to another, but passing through heaven on the way.

GRAPEVINE, TEXAS

Dear Close Personal Friends of the Briggs Family,
Since our last Christmas letter, Grandpa got
his harness straightened, his prostate scraped, and a whole new
set of teeth! Congratulations, Grandpa, we'll keep you up and
running as long as we can afford it!

Some of you know that last summer Cyndi Lynn Briggs,
fourth child of Asa Briggs, and her eighteen-year-old daughter,
Traci Swope, disappeared from Ridgmar Mall in Fort Worth
while shopping for foundation garments. We hear so many stories these days about kidnapping and crime and the sad world
we live in, that we were all real worried. But then Cyndi Lynn
and Traci turned up in Wichita, Kansas, with lucrative divorce

settlements. Congratulations, girls, and best holiday wishes in sunny Las Vegas!

Here in Grapevine the family is planning a traditional Christmas, even though Chief Nogales says he doesn't want anybody getting as drunk as we did last year. Bobo is stealing us a tree from the ranch where he works. Wanda is making a pie in the shape of Texas, except for the curvy parts down by Laredo where it's too hard. Little Beth Ellen is bringing two of her friends from the orphanage to show them how "real people" live. We'll be sure to give both of them a nickel. You know, sometimes we need to pause and reflect on the people that God decided to make less fortunate than us because they refuse to work.

There's not much to say about the lawsuit. Buster Crowell still claims our clothesline was slapping up against his satellite dish and destroying the reception, but Uncle Cletis says he never should of installed it by the sandbox anyhow, because that's a "public abuse area" covered by the Lake Grapevine Trailer Park Residents Association agreement that we all signed back in 1984 so that Floyce Stinson couldn't put another hot tub in the trailer she was using for ten-dollar massages. Two weeks ago somebody put a dent in our toolshed. We're not blaming Buster for doing it cause there weren't any witnesses.

Houston Weeks got all the way to state this year in high school rodeo, but the judges cheated him out of first when his first bull had a hurt hind leg and they wouldn't disqualify him and give Houston a normal fair animal. Houston should be getting out of Baylor Hospital next June. That boy always did know how to get off school!

Aunt Jessie bought $788 worth of magazines from a man in

a Delta 88. They sent her all the magazines on the same day. Amy might use em for a collage they have to make at school.

They finally fired Otis Clendenon from the vet when they found out he was operating on crippled cows and he didn't ever get him a license. He said he went to A&M but nobody ever checked his papers. Bill Denny wants to know if Otis has to pay for the cows, but our lawyer, Bubba Barclay, says once a cow is dead and sold, you can't make a man pay the difference between a dead or a live cow unless you can prove the dead cow wouldn't of been dead unless Otis stuck a surgical clamp up its nose or something equally stupid, since they were crippled cows to begin with, and before Otis come along and said he could operate on em, we used to shoot em anyhow. Bubba's representing Otis on a commission basis.

Margaret Stephenson lost 240 pounds on one of those new Oprah Winfrey diets. Keep up the good work, Margaret!

Margaret Stephenson's mother, Emily Stephenson, will be accepting Coconut Malt-O-Meal Fruitcake orders until February first this year, because of last year when she couldn't sell em all by Christmas.

Ruth Briggs, on the Lubbock side of the family, won a trip to Amarillo to try out for *Wheel of Fortune*. She plans to leave Jess at home and make a week of it! Remember, Ruth, always buy an E!

We have so much to be thankful for during this time of year when the baby Jesus was born and we all get sick on tequila. Most families aren't as fortunate as us Briggses, so let's remember all the other families and make sure we keep em down where they can't hurt us. God bless every one of you—that's in the family, that is!

NO SPRECHEN ZEE AMERICAN?

Slopehead Connecticut debutantes with gold bangly bracelets are carrying signs all across the country about how English should be the official language, *no habla Esspanyolay*, *no sprechen zee Doitchee-voo*, and, of course, no *Tsing Tao Van Nuys*. They're afraid that if we let all these Swahilis come over here and talk to one another so *we can't understand what they're planning*, then the whole country will get taken over by terrorists and people who'll work in the silicon-chip factory for less than the minimum wage. They're passing laws all over the lot about this stuff, like in Monterey Park, California, where all the trustees of the library got kicked out for buying magazines like *Pakistani Monthly* and *Urdu!*

And now they want everybody that gets across the Rio Grande to have to take a citizenship test in English and prove they know at least three episodes of *I Love Lucy* by heart.

I got the solution for this deal.

First, if we're all gonna speak the same language, and we're gonna force everybody to take a *test* in the language, then let's make it fair. Let's all start from the same place. Let's make it a language *nobody* knows yet.

Let's make it Icelandic, the official language of Iceland.

Now I know what you're thinking. You're thinking, "Hey, wait a minute, Joe Bob, that would be unfair for people that emigrated here from Iceland!"

No, it wouldn't, for two reasons. Uno, there's only 243,000 people in Iceland anyhow. And two-o, all of em *already* had to get through the Icelandic public schools, where you're required to learn *four* foreign languages, *including* English. These are the Big Leagues in the spicka-yo-language department. They've already played in the Super Bowl. We can let em in with no problem.

Now it's our turn.

Can you say *Vestur-Skaftafellssysla*? I bet you can!

And I don't wanna hear any wimp excuses, either, like, "I'm working sixteen hours a day at two jobs and I don't have *time* to learn a language."

You should of thought of that on the day you decided to be an American. Course, most of you never *decided* to be Americans at all, did you? You just kinda *claimed* that you did some day after you figured out you were born here. So you're even *worse* than the ones who *chose* to live here.

"I don't have enough money for the lessons."

But you have enough money for *Christmas presents*, don't

you? It's funny how you seem to come up with those bucks for *cigarettes*, isn't it? Nyah nyah nyah, etc. etc. etc.

"But Grandma's eighty-four years old and she can't be expected to learn how to conjugate Nordic verbs or identify the glaciers of the Reykjanessvaedhi range."

Fine. Grandma doesn't have to vote. That's her privilege.

"It's unfair. It's arbitrary. You just chose a language out of the blue. My life has nothing to do with the life of Skallagrimur Kveldulfsson."

That's where you're wrong. I already explained this. *English* is the one we chose out of the blue. Nobody ever *decided* to speak English. In fact, we *hated* the English when the country got started. It was just the language that we happened to be speaking at the time—some of us, anyhow. Icelandic, on the other hand, is one that we *chose* to speak, the one that *proves* your desire to *really* be an American.

"I'm not good at languages. I could never even remember the difference between Keflavik and Syedhisfjordhur."

Guess you better head on back to Vladivostok or wherever. Don't you realize we're doing this for your *own good?* Don't you realize that if you're gonna function in an Icelandic-speaking society, you *must* speak Icelandic?

"Okay, I'll do it, but only if you let me have at least five or six years to get really good at it."

What! Bilingual education?! Do you realize how that makes you *soft* and *lazy* inside? How it just maintains you at your current level? How it's just an excuse for *never* learning Icelandic?

"What makes you such an expert at this?"

Only one thing.

I already speak Icelandic.

S ome guys at the University of Utah with really
bad haircuts say they've "induced fusion" in a
bottle. What this means is, they've rammed a couple atoms
together like Silly Putty basketballs, and they think the atoms
will get real jumpy and juiced up and pretty soon you can stick
a couple of University of Utah atoms in a transistor radio and
pick up stations in Bucharest. Which is all pretty interesting, but
it's even *more* interesting that when these two guys figured it
out, they didn't just send off their experiments to other scientists
around the world. They held a big press conference in Salt Lake
City. One guy said it was so "we could improve the image of
Utah and encourage growth."

Of course, we can all see the logic of this. My friend Lester Rollins was about to open up a new Roto-Rooter franchise in Houston, but as soon as he heard about "cold fusion," he said, "You know what, Joe Bob? I'm doing *my* plumbing in Utah." Up at the University of Arkansas, the entire Sigma Nu fraternity interrupted "Pig Trough Weekend" to announce they would all be transferring to the University of Utah. And durn near every Radio Shack salesman and deputy sheriff between here and Alabama started looking into real estate prices in Provo.

In fact, other universities around the world were so ticked off about the U of U getting all the "fusion publicity" that there's gonna be a whole slew of counter–press conferences this week.

At the University of Heidelberg, theologians will announce that the book of Jeremiah was actually written in 750 B.C., and not 627 B.C., as previously believed. "Our team has also uncovered strong evidence," said one scholar, "that Jeremiah's actual name was Klondike, but we're waiting on further research before we say that for sure." University officials are hoping the announcement will help attract American servicemen to the boutiques selling antique Bavarian beer steins in the new "Old Heidelberg" shopping district.

Meanwhile, at Cambridge University in England, scholars are on the verge of announcing a new city in ancient Mesopotamia. "We're calling it Al-akhen'notten-hatenteparup," said Dr. Phineas Strop, Associate Professor of Near Eastern Antiquities. "That's the name we find on all the inscriptions. The city is located in modern-day Iraq. We were very fortunate. An Iraqi heat-seeking missile was aimed at Iran, but instead it blew up right there in the middle of the army and uncovered this previously unknown treasure city of the Mongol king Urken. We're very proud. All of us here at the college call ourselves Urksters now." The university's chancellor will also appear at the news conference, hoping to use the publicity about Al-akhen'nottenhatenteparup to influence parliament to locate a new coal-fired generating plant in the Cambridge area.

At Purdue University, a news conference will be held within two weeks to announce the development of a new syntheticsoybean substitute that has resulted in 50 percent more muscle mass in polled Hereford cattle. "They eat this stuff like cotton candy," said Homer Withrow, head of the School of Agricultural Sciences. "We had a heifer out here the other day, had to yank her head out of the trough. She was about to explode she was suckin it down so fast." The mayor of West Lafayette, Indiana, will appear at the news conference to announce plans for a new "Hefty Heifer" tourist development, and to express hope that Sony will now decide to locate its new microchip factory in Indiana.

Finally, scholars at the University of Nevada at Las Vegas, stunned by such a publicity coup in a neighboring state, are holding a press conference to announce that Norman "Footsie" Pettus, an assistant professor in the Physical Education Department, has developed a new weight-training device that can add five inches to the average basketball player's upper thighs. "You can kiss the Nautilus equipment good-bye when they see this baby," said Pettus. "We're in the early stages of testing, but after six weeks' work on this machine, we had one ball player who could do a triple somersault and slam-dunk on the way down. Some of the boys have been asking me if they can jump over the backboard from the backside and slam-dunk with their *feet*, but I'm not prepared to authorize that yet." Several casino owners will appear at the news conference with Pettus to send a clear message to the world that "Las Vegas is more than gambling.

We have a fine university here, a fine town, and this is a prime location for any research and development company seeking quiet and solitude for its employees." And later in the week, the governor of Nevada will announce double odds on blackjack and baccarat for any corporation relocating to southern Nevada within the next six months.

Even with all this academic activity, I still doubt anybody will be able to catch up to the U of U. I have to admit, I was so impressed by cold fusion that I immediately checked into strip–shopping center leases in Ogden. Sorry to tell you this, but all the speculators have already moved in and opened up Baskin-Robbins franchises. I'm afraid Utah will never be the same.

There's this newspaper out in Orange County, California, that's decided to send reporters over to the mall. It's all part of their idea they need to be more hip and modern and "lively," and they don't even talk about their "readers" anymore. That's a dirty word. They have "customers." And they need to "connect on a personal basis" with those customers. And so one thing they're planning to do is assign a reporter to cover the mall.

This guy, or gal, is gonna be the Chief Shopping Mall Correspondent. Anything that goes on in the malls, they're gonna be right on top of it. L.A. Gear gets a new line of chartreuse jogging suits and—wham!—Orange County "customers" have the story the next day. Western Auto starts putting swingsets out on the sidewalk, and twelve hours later, Orange County *knows* it. All the Anaheim junior-high drill teams set up booths on the terrace level to collect money for cystic fibrosis—get out the 72-point Bodoni Bold headline type! That World War III story can wait till later.

In other words, *my* kind of newspaper! I want this job. I want this job so bad I'm submitting the following sample articles I would write as the Orange County Chief Mall Correspondent.

1. Dateline South Coast Plaza, Costa Mesa: "Yesterday there were some real *mean* guys from El Lay hanging around Spencer Gifts. They had a lot of zippers on their jackets and they threw the paper from their Mrs. Field's chocolate-chip cookies right down on the floor. Cissy Cameron wanted to talk to them, but her mom wouldn't let her. The one named Josh spit on the Kinney's Shoe Store window and watched it drip down. It was gross! Mrs. Cameron said Josh might get in trouble."

2. Dateline Fashion Island, Newport Beach: "The escalator in front of Sears broke down, and everybody had to take the elevator that handicapped people and real old people use. They said it would be fixed tomorrow. A lot more people had to walk by the pet store. Somebody stole a rubber teething bone."

3. Dateline South Bay Galleria, Hermosa Beach: "Radio Shack just got 970 new Sony Walkmans in for high-school graduation week."

4. Dateline Park Plaza, Escondido: "Lisa, Sheila, and Teri, three of the college girls that were working in costume jewelry at Mervyn's, quit last week because they said they couldn't stand hearing the same Christmas music over and

over again all day long. They never did get along with the assistant manager, Jerry, anyway. They all thought he was a jerk, and he was always making these *sexual* comments about Teri's skirts. He's kind of a jerk."

5. Dateline Big Town, Riverside: "They had a clown giving away free balloons yesterday, but the helium machine broke down and three little kids started crying. Asked to comment, Assistant Mall Manager Stuart Simpson said, "Big Town will not be repeating the clown promotion in the future until we have performed proper maintenance on the helium-injection tanks. We regret any inconvenience this may have caused to the mothers of the Inland Empire."

6. Dateline Sherman Oaks Galleria: "The lasagna at Luby's Cafeteria had big brown spots on the noodles. I took mine back, and they gave me some turkey and dressing and a free slice of garlic bread."

7. Dateline Beverly Center, Beverly Hills: "They have these leather purses at the Broadway Department Store that have rhinestones on the front and a gold clasp and a little chain, but you can't tell what they look like in the store. I mean, they *might* be really classy-looking purses if you had *just* the right dress, but when you're looking at them there on the purse counter, with all the *other* purses, you just can't tell. It's too bad you can't take one home and put on your evening dress and then see how the purse looks with it. You've got to describe the dress to the saleslady, and the saleslady always acts like she knows *exactly* what you're talking about, but you know she doesn't. They're such liars. And so you know you're gonna buy it, and then you know you're gonna hate yourself later."

8. Dateline Wonder West Mall, San Bernardino: "Nobody

wants these Hairy Krishna people hanging around all the time, especially when they're always *eyeing* you every time you walk by B. Dalton's. If you think the Hairy Krishnas should be kicked out of the mall, call this newspaper's special 976 number listed below on this page. Results of this poll are unscientific, but we'll use it to try to get em kicked out anyway."

What do you think?

Do I get the job?

Please.

They're closing down the Trader Vic's in New York City with the Zambooli spears on the walls and the totem poles that look like Charles Manson's wood-shop project and the bamboo chairs and the little umbrellas on the table made by white slavers in the Philippines. And do you know *why* they're doing this?

Because Donald Trump says it's "tacky."

The Trumpster bought the Plaza Hotel, and so he's kicking Vic's out of the basement, where it's been for the last twenty-five years, and where I occasionally like to hang out when forced to put on a gas mask and enter midtown Manhattan.

This is a *historical* place. It's the kind of place you go when you need to disappear from the face of the planet for five or six hours at a time. I went in there one night with some crew members from a cable-TV show, and we ordered the famous Samoan Fog Cutter, chased it with a Menehune Juice with complimentary South Pacific tribal-goddess-on-a-stick, and then decided to try the Fuji Fruity Flaming Cootie. In case you've never been there, after two Samoan Fog Cutters, they'll throw in a Fuji Fruity Flaming Cootie free of charge for anybody who can successfully order one.

Anyhow, the whole idea of the place is that you go into this Gilligan's Island fern bar decorated with Eskimo artifacts where it takes about forty-five minutes for your eyes to adjust to the blackness, and then you throw back a few of these brain-scramblers that basically taste like Gatorade with a little lime juice mixed in, and before you know what's happening, against your will, without realizing where you are, you're *ordering a poo-poo tray.*

At most times of the day and night, under normal conditions, just the *idea* of a poo-poo tray would make it necessary to poo-poo. A poo-poo tray is a Lazy Susan with a flaming barbecue pit in the middle, and around the outside of it are chunks of bloody beef on a tongue depressor, egg rolls that feel like giant ball bearings, shrimp with so much batter around em that they look like they've been blown up with a bicycle pump, and other stuff that you never can decide *what* it is, except it starts to taste okay if you pour some liquid-hydrogen Chinese mustard on it.

Sometimes, if you have a large enough group and you've been through the Trader Vic's experience enough times, there will even be wise guys who say, "What do you say? Should we go for a poo-poo?" (Veterans will simply say, "Time to poo-poo?")

And then, *regardless* of what anyone says, within ten minutes there will be at least one, but more likely six, poo-poo trays on the table, all served by a smiling Chinese guy who keeps saying, "You want poo-poo? Share poo-poo or separate poo-poo?"

But by then it's too late. To cut down on the poo-poo aftertaste, you're gonna need to order two or three Bahama Mamas and a couple of Tahiti Funkmasters. You have now reached the crucial moment in any Trader Vic's experience. You will start *examining* the objects on the walls. You will be extremely interested in the dugout canoe over the entrance, not to mention the thatched-hut bar. You will consider these objects, and they will become the most beautiful objects in the world to you. You will start spouting everything you know about why Marlon Brando moved to Tahiti. You will recite scenes from *Mutiny on the Bounty*. You will start talking about how Asian women have more sensuous bodies than American women.

"I think it's really neat in here."

You see what's happening? The first person to utter the words "I think it's really neat in here" can *not* be allowed to drive home, under any circumstances. He can't even be allowed to head for the subway by himself. And there's only one thing that can save him: The Peking duck.

"Peking duck for six?"

The Chinese guy is at your elbow before you've even said the words out loud.

You are now in for the long-haul Trader Vic's experience. You will never be the same again. You will spend $397 this night for "the greatest friends I've ever had in the world." Your American Express bill will come in two envelopes next month. But you don't care, because you have vanished off the face of the earth.

And Donald Trump calls this tacky?

Get the man something to *do* with his life.

DEATH ROW U.S.A.

Y ou ever meet a Death Row lawyer?

They're nervous. They're crotchety. They're almost always smokers. They don't have cocktails. They have "belts." They start a lot of conversations with, "You know what they tried to do to me today?"

Death-house lawyers talk about "my guy" a lot. "My guy" is the man who has an official "kill date." Usually the lawyers don't even like "my guy." "My guy" tends to be a surly, ungrateful killer who either a) begs the lawyer to do the impossible, or b) screams at the lawyer because he's not doing the impossible.

"My guy says he wants to write a letter to the governor," the lawyer will tell you. "He wants to fire me and write his own letter to the governor. I can see it now. 'Dear Ignorant Jerkhead Slimeball Politician, Let me outta here.' "

Death Row lawyers don't take many vacations. They rarely get paid. They're always accused of being arrogant. Judges develop a distaste for dealing with em. And do you know why?

Because they don't care what the law is.

They just wanna win.

They wanna save some guy's lousy dead-end life who, once he gets his sentence commuted, is never gonna call the lawyer again or give him a second thought. And maybe, somewhere down the line, some court will award the Death Row lawyer about one tenth of what his fees should be, and the rest of the money will never be paid.

These guys aren't arrogant. They're scared. They're even more scared than the judge or jury that sentenced the guy to death. Those people had well-defined *rules* to follow. But the lawyer has nothing to follow but his gut, which is telling him, "If I do my job right, no man can be put to death by the government in America."

There's only one time the lawyer doesn't come into the office—on the day after an execution.

The Chief Justice of the Supreme Court doesn't like these Death Row lawyers. He thinks they're slowing down the process of killing people. He thinks they're wasting valuable time that the courts could be spending on more important things than the life or death of a killer. And so Chief Justice Rehnquist has been spending a lot of time trying to get the law changed. He wants a limit on the number of times a lawyer can file a "habeas corpus" petition. He wants that limit to be one time. If you don't win that one time, then you go back to prison and wait to die.

"Habeas corpus" is a good name for it, because in Latin it

means "You have a body." And so lawyers file these petitions that start out, "You have a body on Death Row, and that body should be somewhere else." Then the lawyer shows *why* the guy should be somewhere else, and the court has to answer each question. The "whys" usually go like this:

1. My guy had an incompetent lawyer.
2. My guy had a prejudiced jury.
3. My guy has new evidence.
4. My guy is crazy.
5. My guy was crazy at the time he did it.
6. My guy wasn't charged with the thing he was convicted for. The grand jury screwed up the indictment.
7. My guy was damaged by media publicity that made it impossible for him to have a fair trial.
8. My guy didn't do anything near as bad as somebody else who got off scot-free.
9. My guy was arrested improperly.
10. My guy was searched improperly.
11. They didn't read my guy his rights.
12. My guy was questioned without a lawyer being there.
13. My guy was held in jail too long without the chance to talk to his lawyer.
14. My guy poses no danger to society, because he's turned religious.
15. Two of the witnesses that identified my guy said he was five-ten, but he's six feet tall.
16. One witness said he had bushy eyebrows, but he has thin ones.
17. One witness said my guy ordered her to get down on the floor. But three years later, at the trial, the same witness said she was ordered to stand against the wall.

18. There are contradictions in what every single witness said about my guy, so you should let him go.

19. Nobody ever found a gun.

20. Nobody ever proved he was at the place where the murder happened.

21. The prosecuting attorney called my guy "the slimiest of the slimy," arousing the prejudice of the jury.

22. My guy was crazy at the time, but by the time you appointed a psychiatrist, he wasn't crazy anymore.

23. My guy wasn't crazy at the time, but he's crazy now, so he can't have meaningful discussions with his lawyer, and so he can't file a fair appeal.

24. My guy's lawyer was crazy.

25. I'm incompetent.

26. I'm crazy.

27. He didn't do it.

28. What if he didn't do it?

29. Mr. Justice Rehnquist, please have mercy.

30. Governor, please have mercy.

31. The method of execution is "cruel and unusual."

32. Governor, please have mercy.

33. The prisoner was not properly informed of his place and time of execution.

34. Governor, this man has a family.

35. The prisoner has changed the lives of many other inmates on Death Row. He is fully rehabilitated.

36. Governor, I'm begging you.

37. We have new evidence.

38. Please, Governor, be a man.

39. At least let the man die with dignity, in an upright position, not lying on a gurney with a needle in his arm.

And then there's no need for any more "habeas corpus" petitions, because there is no longer any body.

Now why would Chief Justice Rehnquist dislike this tedious, time-consuming process? Maybe because it demonstrates a thousand tiny flaws in the system. Maybe because it shows us how many eyewitnesses have been wrong, how many guys who are certifiably crazy have been executed, how many mistakes the government can make when they're dealing with something as unreliable as human judgment.

Fortunately for him, Chief Justice Rehnquist doesn't have to make that last phone call to the guy's family. The death-house lawyer gets to do that, too.

PART 4

THE REST OF THE WORLD

(WE KNOW IT EXISTS, BECAUSE WE SEE IT ON CNN)

YASSIR ARAFAT AND BOBBY BOHANNON

Yassir Arafat reminds me of this kid I used to know name of Bobby Bohannon. Bobby Bohannon lived down at the end of Thirty-fourth Street in Texarkana, Arkansas, where the road petered out and became gravel and then mud and then a soybean field. Bobby's was the last house before the soybean field, and it wasn't much of a house. Didn't even have a screen door on it, and his concrete porch had a crack three feet wide where we'd spray the water hose in the summer to try to make snakes come out so we could kill em. Bobby's father, Mr. Bohannon, would come out on the porch ever once in a while and threaten to whale the tar out of us if we didn't get off his lot. Mr. Bohannon had a rubber hand—he lost it in Korea or something—and we were afraid of that rubber hand, like if you touched it, grease would come off on your skin.

Bobby Bohannon was the meanest kid on Thirty-fourth Street. He could grab you around the neck from behind and push you facedown in the dirt and plant both knees on your back before you knew what was happening, and it wasn't so much the pain of it as the fact that you knew you couldn't do a thing about it. You couldn't talk to Bobby Bohannon because he wouldn't talk back to you. You couldn't fight with him because you knew he could whip you. You could get so mad that you'd get three or four guys to help you, and maybe you could jump him when he wasn't looking, but he'd fight so hard that, even if you finally got him down on the ground and all four of you sat on him, you'd only just *technically* win, because he'd just keep spitting right back at you through his bloody mouth, and you'd end up feeling worse than he would. And so we all developed the theory that anybody who been beat on all his life with a rubber hand is gonna be pure-dee mean, and there's nothing you can do about it except stay out of his way.

And then one day a deputy sheriff came to Bobby Bohannon's house and put an eviction notice on the door, and we thought everything was gonna get better since that meant Mr. Bohannon would have to move four blocks away to the concrete-block apartments where you'd have to move when you got a divorce or you lost your job or you didn't want people in Texarkana to know you were a homosexual. And that's sure enough what happened, only it wasn't the end of Bobby Bohannon.

A new family moved into the Bohannon house, the Jacksons, and Bobby Bohannon found out about it and started coming back into the neighborhood and beating up the Jackson brothers even though they were all at least three grades younger than him. And since Bobby had been held back at least two grades that we know of, that meant five years' difference. So he'd wait till he saw Danny Jackson walking home from Vacation Bible School and he'd grab him by the shoulder, rip up the Crayola drawings he was taking home to his mother, maybe throw his lunch box in the creek, and then beat him on the ears until he started to bleed. And then Danny Jackson would tell his mother, and if it was bad enough, Bobby Bohannon would have to go to the juvenile detention center for a while.

Everybody agreed that Bobby Bohannon should go to the detention center for a while. It wasn't Danny Jackson's fault that Mr. Bohannon lost his house. It wasn't anybody else's fault that Bobby Bohannon got beat with a rubber hand every night of his life. We didn't have to let him beat up on our friends just because he had a hard life. Every one of us had *something* hard happening in our life.

And then one year, when Bobby Bohannon was about twenty years old, he came back to the neighborhood from getting out of Cummins Prison Farm where he'd been sent for the last two years, and I happened to see him on the street, and I was surprised to see how *small* he was. Now that we were both pretty much grown up, he wasn't any bigger than I was. And Bobby didn't jump on me or nothing. He just said, "I was thinking about playing some ball."

We never did let Bobby Bohannon play baseball with us, because the Jackson brothers played.

"My daddy died," he told me.

Somehow I knew it was okay to let him play. He wouldn't be hassling the Jackson brothers anymore. Bobby Bohannon didn't have to say much for you to know he wasn't talking about baseball.

"I reckon we could get up a game," I told him.

But, of course, the ball game never happened. No parent in his right mind was gonna let his kid play baseball with Bobby Bohannon or even spend time around that boy. Bobby was pure-dee mean. If he was coming around, acting nice, he must be up to something. If he wanted to be friends with everybody, he should have thought of that before he started beating up on little Danny Jackson. You can't just up and say "I'm sorry" and expect us to forget all those years. I guess you can pretty much imagine what all the grown-ups were saying.

Myself, I would of enjoyed playing a little baseball with Bobby.

Anyhow, like I was saying, Yassir Arafat reminds me of Bobby Bohannon.

T he pygmies don't want to be called pygmies anymore. They have a good point. The men are four-
foot-ten and the women are four-foot-four, and they're *sick and
tired* of these stupid stereotypes spread by ignorant people who
think they are short. An incredibly tall spokesman talked about
it to a *National Geographic* film crew, said that pygmy prejudice is rampant, and made an international appeal by staring
straight into the cameraman's kneecap and demanding that people stop making pygmy jokes.

I understand his point. I fully sympathize with the needs,
hopes, and aspirations of people who are . . . well, I started to
say small . . . people who are . . . compact and dignified. No,

that's not quite it. People who are shaped by a loving God into the form He desires for them, a shape that resembles a giant Betsy Wetsy doll.

One of the points they're making is that pygmies are "normal-sized" if you look at them in *their* culture, where *everybody* is a pygmy. Of course, if we're gonna do that, we need to kick out the *National Geographic* film crews, also known by the pygmies as Giant British Twit-Monsters from the North. One reason we think the pygmies are so short is that English guys in baggy sweaters and Hush Puppies are always standing around making them feel like cockroach people. *Stop taking pictures* of them. That'll help. And if you *do* take pictures of them, take some Barbie dollhouse furniture with you to make em feel at home in front of the camera.

The pygmies, unfortunately, aren't the only people in the world suffering from mindless, ignorant cultural discrimination. Consider these cruel stereotypes:

1. The Irish are actually sober 20 percent of the time, but does anybody ever write about *that*?

2. There are two Norwegians in Minnesota who do *not* wear baggy pants and scratch themselves in public. Try to find *that* story in the national media.

3. The French are actually very nice people. Most of them prefer that you do *not* leave a tip. They would be embarrassed to take your money. In fact, you'll get better service if you do *not* tip them.

4. Italian women remain slender after that sixth child.

5. Okay, yes, it's true that Texans consume more Jack Daniel's whiskey than any state in America and more than any foreign country. But what you *don't* know is that we also consume more Bloody Marys *at breakfast* than any

state in America. So it kind of evens out, when you have all the facts.

6. Koreans are excellent drivers. Most freeway accidents involving people named "Kim" are caused by guardrails that break off too easily.

7. Mexicans are perfectly capable of electing politicians who aren't crooks. Look at Tomás Javier Pena, mayor of Zapatano, a village of some thirty-four people in the north-western corner of Tamaulipas. The man has never taken a bribe in his life. Do you see *him* on *60 Minutes?*

8. People in Colombia hate cocaine. In fact, if a man comes into a restaurant and someone thinks he's about to pay for his meal with *drug money,* no one will take it. If he orders a $10,000 bottle of wine, they won't even sell it to him. This drug thing is blown all out of proportion. It's just the action of a few meanies that nobody else will have anything to do with.

9. Swedes are not blond anymore. They *used* to be blond, but people made fun of them for being blond, and they're sick and tired of it. Most of them are "undark," and they would appreciate it if the international media would adopt that term for Swedish hair color.

10. Germans stopped being stocky in 1957. It was a carry-over from the Nazi era, but since that time stockiness has been outlawed in all states except the one that recently elected eleven right-wingers to Parliament. You can tell they're Nazis because they're stocky. In fact, there weren't any Nazis in Germany. There never were. It was one of those stereotypes the world *wanted* to believe about them.

11. Nobody in Bangladesh is poor.

12. The Russians hate vodka.

And, of course, we could go on and on with this, but let me leave you with just one thought. Think of this the next time you're about to make some mindless cultural or ethnic joke that's based on nothing more than your own distorted view of the world:

People used to say all Americans could joke about one another without taking it personally. Obviously, this was a cruel stereotype.

HASTA LA DINERO

A few years back, we had a bunch of dimwit bankers in Texas who had so much oil money pouring in they started making car loans to javelina hogs and building condos in Deadhorse, Alaska, because "we can't have all this money laying around here." And then OPEC fell apart and all the oil prices went down the toilet and now all those guys work at Denny's and all the banks in Dallas have big signs on em like THE NORTH CAROLINA STATE SAVINGS AND LOAN BANK OF CANADA. The whole city's been sold off for scrap.

Anyhow, those guys might have been missing a few face cards, but there's one thing the Texas bankers would have never, ever done—loan money to the bozos in South America. It took a New Yorker to think this idea up.

I mean, what were these guys thinking when they ran up a

$277 *billion* bill? That if they didn't pay up, we could send a bunch of guys from Color Tyme TV Rental down there to repossess downtown Santiago? What do they do all day up on the international floor at Chase Manhattan?

"Hey, Frank, get on the other line! It's Carlos! Yeah, I think we've got good news. Carlos! Baby! Talk to me! I tell you what. Pay down a little principal this month on the nuclear-reactor loan in the Amazon jungle, and I'll let the interest ride on the twenty-seven hydroelectric projects. But, Carlos, listen to me, this is your *last chance*. I'm afraid my next step will be your lawyer talking to my lawyer. It is? Are you serious? Great! Hey, Frank, the check's coming in on tonight's Pan Am flight from Montevideo. Great, Carlos, and by the way—say hi to Maria and all the little ones for me. Be careful driving home. You still got terrorists down there? Bummer. *Hasta* later, man."

What I'm saying is, you show these loans to a Texas banker, and he would have said something like, "I don't know. I'm just not sure you can lend 277 billion bucks to somebody with an income of 3,700 cruzeiros a year. What's that come out to, 3,700 cruzeiros? About fourteen cents? I think the debt payments need to be a little less than seven trillion percent of your monthly income."

But the New York banks, they *wanted* this business. They made trips down there to beg the president of Brazil to take *their* money, not somebody else's. And then, when they were leaving, they said something like, "Now, Mr. Morales, just exactly what was it you were planning to use this money for?"

"Uh, er . . . highways. Yeah, that's it. Highways."

"Great! Highways! Well, I hope you build some beautiful highways."

"Or maybe power plants."

"Power plants are good. We like power plants. And you would repay the loan with money coming in from people's electric bills, right? By the way, that's an extremely nice watch you're wearing."

"Bally of Switzerland. *Muito obrigato.* Yes, we'll pay it back very quickly. And feedlots for cattle—we'll build a lot of those, too."

"Great, that's good. I'm a steak-and-potatoes man myself. Well, I've got to run. I know you've got a plane to catch, too. Remember, next year I'll try to bring that four percent interest down to a more reasonable rate."

"We would appreciate it. We are a very poor country."

"I know that, Señor Alfonsín. Would you like to ride to the airport with me?"

"Are you on the Zurich flight?"

"No, I'm going back to the office in New York."

"That's all right then. I'll have the limousine and the honor guard drop me off."

"Fine. And next time let's talk about some more loans. Maybe some housing. I was noticing on the ride in, you guys could use some home improvement loans, especially down there on Cardboard Row. And some of those tummies are running on empty, too, aren't they?"

"Three percent next time."

"*Quatro, mieu amigo,* best I can do."

And then they would bear-hug each other and the guy from New York would go home and three years later they would be sitting in the bank president's office, going, "I don't know, it just seemed like a great idea, he was building dams and bridges and highways—I figured the tolls and the electric bills, he'd have some money rolling in. Maybe we could repo thirty or forty of the Jaguars."

Maybe the Texas guys were colossal idiots. Maybe they loaned money to grade-school dropouts with three-foot pompadours who wanted to build apartments in Boise for lesbians. But every single buck they poured out got spent in America, by somebody trying to make *more* money, that he would *also* spend in America. The Texans didn't build any concrete shells in the jungle or pay for any lobster dinners in Geneva. It took the geniuses on Wall Street to do that. Now they say they need help from the government.

Let em fry.

Let em fry like they let the Texans fry.

PART 5

THINGS WE DO
TO FORGET
WE'RE DOOMED

ABDOMENIZING

My Abdomenizer came in the mail so fast I didn't even have to wait four to six weeks. "It's here! It's here! The Abdomenizer is here!" I yelled out to Wanda Bodine. Wanda was with me the night I bought it. We were watching *Gorgeous Ladies of Rasslin,* and the bimbo in the pink swimsuit came on, doing her Abdomenizer sit-ups, and I said to Wanda, "You know, this commercial's been on for ninety-seven years. There must be something to it."

And Wanda was skeptical. She said, "That thing looks like one of those cheap plastic sleds for sliding down hills in the snow."

"It can't be cheap plastic, even though it *looks* like cheap plastic, because it costs $19.95."

And Wanda said, "Not that you couldn't use a little Abdomenizing."

And so that was it. I called the 800 number in Canton, Ohio, and told em, "I want an Abdomenizer," and the lady took down the information and said, "Do you think you might want *two* Abdomenizers? We'll give you the second one for $9.95."

I hung up the phone and said, "Yep, cheap plastic."

One thing you should know, if you're thinking about getting an Abdomenizer, is that it comes in a giant white box that has ABDOMENIZER written all over it and advertising like "Firms Stomach!" and "Safer for Your Lower Back!" and "As Seen on TV!" and a big picture of the Abdomenizer so that everybody in your neighborhood will know you ordered it even before you get it. Scrim Wilks saw the mailman carrying it around and he called me up.

"Joe Bob, your *Abdomenizer* is here." And then he couldn't stop laughing. He kept saying "Abdomenizer" over and over again in a way that sounded like "You hopeless ignorant beer-belly dufus." It's humiliating.

So I said to Wanda, "That's okay, if it doesn't work out, we'll use it for a sled."

This was before we opened it up and read the silver sticker next to the Abdomenizer Carrying Handle, which is a square cut out of the plastic.

"NOTICE," the sticker said. "*This unit is not to be used as a sled or otherwise misused.*"

I'm not kidding. They *know* that people order em as sleds.

But anyhow, I started getting real excited about changing my life with exercise when I read the instruction booklet for "Abdomenizer: The Intelligent Sit-up," and it started off with about seventeen safety warnings, including "Recommended maximum user weight: 300 pounds" and "Instructions for Full Hips." (You get some old belts out of your closet and hook em in the hand holes so you don't break your hands with your hips while using the Abdomenizer.)

Finally we got down to the nitty-gritty: "Sit on the Abdomenizer in the area marked SIT HERE."

Sure enough, we found SIT HERE imprinted on the blue plastic like TONKA on a dump truck. So I sat there.

"Your tailbone should be just over the Posturing Seat, also called Sit Here."

I adjusted my tailbone.

"The Sit Here area should be flat to the floor when you are in the full upright position. Place your hands into the handle slots on each side of the ABDOMENIZER."

Then there's a bunch of instructions for fat people on how to work it if they can't get their hands into the handle slots, and then there's some exercise tips, and where to put your feet, and along about page 5, you finally get to actually do your first Abdomenizer sit-up. I gave it everything I had.

"How did that feel?" said Wanda.

"Felt like I was rocking back and forth on a piece of cheap plastic."

"Actually," said Wanda, "you were rocking back and forth on a piece of expensive plastic."

"How long should I do this?" I asked her.

"The book says until you experience momentary, slight abdominal fatigue."

"I experienced abdominal fatigue before I ever got down here."

"Probly time to stop then."

"Good. That was an excellent two-sit-up workout. Don't wanna do too much the first day."

And Wanda said, "Joe Bob, do you realize that for thirty bucks more we could have bought the Easy Glider?"

"I know, but I think we should maintain a healthy perspective and *don't overdo it.*"

"Joe Bob, it's a cheap piece of plastic."

"It is *not* a cheap piece of plastic." I was reading the booklet again. "The Abdomenizer was invented by Dr. Dennis Colonello, D.C., who designed it to produce an automatic pelvic tilt, which better isolates abdominal muscles and makes sit-ups safer for your lower back."

"Right, Joe Bob, it's a crime all those people who *died* last year from doing improper sit-ups."

"If I wanna buy an Abdomenizer . . ."

"That's a moot point, because you already *bought* an Abdomenizer."

". . . then I'll *buy* an Abdomenizer. It's a God-given American right to buy anything on an 800 number you feel like, and it doesn't matter that it cost nineteen ninety-five, it would be worth it if it cost a *hundred* and nineteen ninety-five."

To illustrate my point, I took a running start, jumped three feet in the air, and landed on top of the Abdomenizer. It didn't hurt it a bit.

"You call that cheap plastic? They got *three-hundred-pound women* using these things, with no danger to their lower backs. My stomach already feels better after that workout."

"Which phase of the workout did it for you, Joe Bob? The first sit-up or the second one?"

I can't stand it when Wanda Bodine gets like this, so I told her

I was going out for a while, but she was *not* to use my Abdomenizer. So I drove into Dallas and bought some terry-cloth headbands for my future Abdomenizer workouts. But when I got back, I knew something was wrong by the expression Wanda had on her face.

"I guess I was wrong," she said. "I shouldn't have made such a big deal out of it."

"I accept your apology," I told her.

It wasn't till later that night that I noticed the moisture on the bottom of my Abdomenizer. I could swear she got snow on it.

DEVIL HORN

The tenor saxophone is a huge honking beast of a musical instrument that looks like a cobra that's about to strike. I spent about six years trying to play it—me and Tommy Withrow, the only two white guys in Little Rock, Arkansas, who could swing a tenor side-to-side, arch our backs, high-step, and pop the thing into our mouths right on the first downbeat. We learned this from studying the sax section in the Grambling State University band. If you missed by a half-beat or a half-inch, the tenor sax would dig a two-inch scar in your face. That's why it was so macho.

I was remembering this when Dexter Gordon died the other day, cause me and Tommy Withrow were always trying to play the thing like either Dexter Gordon or John Coltrane. There were sax-playing *wimps* who tried to play like Charlie Parker. Charlie Parker played the little midget alto sax. The thing was so small the neck-strap never cut deep crevices in your neck like the tenor did. You didn't even have to stretch for the lower keys on that baby.

David Sanborn plays an alto sax. You see what I'm talking about? Who wants to look like David Sanborn?

But Dexter Gordon was a macho macho man. You had the idea Dexter owned shotguns. He didn't say much—the sure sign of a *monster* underneath that quiet surface. Dexter's tenor looked *bigger* than everybody else's tenor. He could make sounds like a car horn on that sucker.

The other reason Tommy Withrow and me liked the tenor sax was that all band directors *hate* the tenor sax. The tenor sax is this ugly monster mutant instrument, half brass, half wood-wind, that sounds like what a grizzly bear would wanta say musically. In your average high school band, where you're play-ing Mussorgsky and Bach, the tenor was like a next-door neigh-bor working on his Monster Truck engine all day. I had one band director who forced us to stuff towels in the bells of the sax in order to muffle the sound. The tenor sax never fit in.

And so we were like guerrilla-warfare band nerds, Tommy Withrow and me. We had these giant musical Molotov cock-tails, and we tried to play em so that we put our signature on every single piece. Tommy Withrow could play better than I could, though, so this drove me crazy. All-City Band: Tommy was first chair, I was second. All-Region Band: Tommy was first, I was second. Summer band camp: I beat out Tommy for first chair, but he challenged me during the second week and whipped me in the audition like a sick puppy. It was like he was toying with me, letting me taste *just enough* success so he could explode my head with his gold sax cannon.

I was convinced Tommy Withrow was gonna be the next Dexter Gordon. After a few years of this, I even contented myself with dreaming that I would be his backup horn. Maybe Tommy would have a whole band and I would be the leader of the front-line sax section, and we would all do the Grambling side-to-side swing move on every song.

Tommy was so good he would practice scales with sixteenth notes—*all* the scales, without stopping, on the first try. If you haven't ever played a brass or woodwind instrument, let me put this in perspective. In baseball, it would be like taking ten pitches in batting practice and hitting them all over the center-field fence. In writing, it would be like typing out a novel in a couple weeks and then, when you're finished, going "Oh no, I'll have to change that *one* paragraph."

Tommy was also one of those guys who never had to look at the music. Once he played a piece about three times, he knew the whole thing by heart. This is disgusting.

So, of course, we all knew where Tommy would have to go if he was gonna become the next Dexter Gordon. Only one place that sax-playing teenagers in Little Rock, Arkansas, ever wanted to go. And that was North Texas State University in Denton, where the famous One O'Clock Lab Band played. It was called the One O'Clock Lab Band because it rehearsed every day at 1:00 P.M. The second band, the Two O'Clock, practiced at two, and on down to the Nine O'Clock Lab Band, which was, of course, the bottom of the barrel. But the One O'Clock, the best college jazz band in America, had recording contracts, Grammy Awards, and regular performances with top players like Dizzy Gillespie, Duke Ellington, Doc Severinsen. Jazz composers sometimes wrote original music to be performed only by the One O'Clock Lab Band.

Tommy Withrow was two years ahead of me in school, and so he was the first to try out. He passed the audition and got accepted to North Texas. And then that fall, when he enrolled, he called me to tell me the results of his tryout for the lab band.

"Did you wax em?" I asked him.

"Seven O'Clock."

"What do you mean?"

"First chair in the Seven O'Clock. That's the best I could do."

"Are you telling me fourteen guys beat you?"

"No, twelve guys beat me."

"That's impossible. Can you challenge em?"

"I didn't play that bad."

"That's impossible."

A year later I called him.

"Well?" I said.

"Four O'Clock."

"All right. Better."

"I'm the eighth player, and seven of the guys ahead of me are my age."

"So?"

"So this is as high as I go. Maybe Three O'Clock when I'm a senior."

"Are you sure? What if you practice ten hours a day?"

"*Everybody* at this place practices ten hours a day."

"There's nothing else to do?"

"There's nothing else to do."

I packed up my horn and sold it a little while after that. There are some things that God assigns to other people. Dexter Gordon already had the job.

PRAIRIE-DOG HUNTING

I'll be danged if Bush didn't ban all the AK-47 Kalashnikov semiautomatic assault rifles right in the middle of hunting season, and it stopped an order of forty-five I had come in from Bangkok, and now I'm gonna have to cancel all my hunting trips this year. Usually, around mid-April, thirty or forty of us go out to West Texas and hunt prairie dogs with AK-47s. Last year we bagged about forty-three thousand of the little suckers, but we won't get anywhere near that using conventional weapons. And I'll tell you one goldurn thing, Mr. Bush—if somebody gets hurt out there this year, his blood is on *your* hands.

The truth of the matter is, you *need* an AK-47 these days, or at least an M-1, if you're gonna compete with the modern prairie dog. Three years ago—I'll never forget this—my buddy Vince Gabbert went ahead of us to recon a ridge on our flank, and as soon as he stuck his head up over the crest, a unit of about thirty prairie dogs flung themselves at his face. Fortunately, he was able to squeeze off seven hundred rounds and pretty much turn the pd's into little salad-bar croutons, but he was a shaken man when he worked his way back to base camp.

I want you to think about that, Mr. Bush. You say these weapons aren't needed for sporting. I want you to think about what would have happened to Vince if he hadn't had the needed firepower that day. Would he have a face? Would a .22 have done the same job?

I think not.

With each passing year, the prairie dog turns into a wiser and more dangerous adversary. Sure, in the beginning all they did was burrow little holes in dirt piles. But last season we stumbled onto a village of prairie dogs that was surrounded by triple-strand barbed wire, booby-trapped with slingshot mines. Of course, it was prairie-dog-sized barbed wire, so we were able to step on it and remove the obstacle. But my point is that we have an entrenched and resistant enemy with no interest in Western-style democracy. I don't know if you've ever seen your best friend get a mesquite thorn directly in the cheek from a pd "slinger." But I'll tell you this. Once you see it, you'll never again hesitate to pour twelve hundred rounds of lead into the little furry cheeks of a resisting rodent.

Let me tell you how bad it's gotten. Two years ago, just outside of Whiteflat in Motley County, four of us were ambushed by prairie-dog mortar fire that, as near as we could tell, was being launched from a copse of elm trees. We hit the dirt, covered our heads, and slowly worked our way toward the trees, dragging our bodies along with our elbows. But when we got close, suddenly the firing stopped. There was nothing but silence, for better than fifteen minutes. Then Sam Wilkins, covering our left flank, spotted a single prairie dog. He had moved just beyond the tree line, into the open space in front of us. He stared straight ahead, then slowly, like he was in a trance, he began to dance. It was a weird, mesmerizing dance. If you've ever seen a belly dancer in a Tunisian restaurant—that kind of dance. He had a tiny flute with him. The flute couldn't have been any bigger than a little girl's fingernail. He began to play Ukrainian folk melodies, dancing all the while. None of us said a word. Then Sam Wilkins, without warning, screamed, "He's just shimmied for the last time!" and he squeezed off a terrifying barrage. The dancing, flute-playing prairie dog disintegrated, vanished, blown into a thousand pieces. But Sam had given away our position. Within fifteen minutes all three of my friends were dead. I only managed to survive by rolling down an embankment, abandoning my backpack, and traveling only by night for three days.

I know what happened now.

The prairie dogs were directly underneath us all that time—thousands of them, waiting for us to make one wrong noise. The dancing prairie dog gave his life so that the others might live.

This is not like any enemy man has ever faced.

And they say we don't *need* AK-47s to hunt with.

JOE BOB GOES TO THE TENNIS TOURNAMENT

A lot of people come up to me and they say, "Joe Bob, I been slicin my off-forehand volley when I have to play top-spin at the net," and I have to tell em, I'm sorry, but I can't condone anything that kinky. That's the kind of guy I am. I'll answer durn near any question you got about the game of tennis, specially the stupid questions, but if you're gonna start asking me about overhead slams, I'll send you straight over to Harry Hines Boulevard in Dallas, where you can get any disgusting thing you want for twenty bucks. I can afford to be picky. I don't like to brag, but last year, in competitive Mixed Triples competition, I went as high as number seventeen on the computer. I couldn't play tennis worth a flip, but I learned how to make that computer stand up and do tricks.

Anyhow, not many people in America know about the game of Mixed Triples. It's big in Pakistan and Uruguay, but it never has caught on over here due to the lack of an ESPN contract. But the way it works is like this. Each team is made up of three people—an alleged male, an alleged female, and an Undecided. (They have a variation on this in *East* Pakistan, where they play with a male, a female, and a "surprise guest" who often tries to confuse the opposing players by dressing up as David Bowie. I don't recommend this game for beginners, and so the rest of this article will be concerned with the rules for *Classic* Mixed Triples and not the more complicated "Mixed-up Triples.")

Anyhow, you get a boy, a girl, and a Maybe on each team, and the first thing you do is practice lobbing the ball to the opposing team's Maybe to see if they know how to play tennis. You'd be surprised how much time and strategy this can save if you'll just remember this one simple rule. Then the next thing you do is, the man and woman take their positions like they're gonna play the usual game of wimpola mixed doubles, but the Maybe player, also called the Wild Card Contestant, positions itself directly underneath the judge's chair, as close as possible to the old coot without actually knocking his chair over. (For this technique, refer to my previous article, "Use of the Toppling Linesman Decoy," published in the October 1985 issue of *Melons Monthly* magazine.)

Okay, start playing tennis.

Now we come to the big difference between Mixed Doubles and Mixed Triples. Let's say you're serving. Usually you throw the ball up, hit it over the net, and wait for one of two things to happen: Either the guy hits it back, or the linesman yells "Fow."

I always wondered *why* they yell "Fow." It'd make it a whole lot easier if they'd yell "Fault," like normal people. But they yell "Fow." But in Mixed Triples you don't wait for that call. Server tosses ball. Server hits ball. Wild Card Contestant screams "Fowwwwww!" Now you start to see the possibilities of this game:

Variation Numero Uno: The guy on the other side hears the "Fow," thinks the ball's called out, and hits it lightly to the ball boy. You're up 15–love. This is known as the Natural Fow.

Variation Numero Two-o: The guy hears the "Fow," figures it out, and starts returning everything in sight, no matter what. He gets worn out. The linespeople get P.O.'d at him. He's a basket case. 40–love your way. This is known as the Spiritual Fow.

Variation Numero Three-o: You start screaming "Fow" in a totally random pattern, including while your opponent is sitting on the bench lacing up his shoes. You start doing all kinds of "Fows"—little squeaky midget "Fows," big booming Mr. T "Fows," and obnoxious Van Halen heavy-metal "Fows." If you're lucky, he'll instruct his Wild Card Contestant to start "Fowing" right back at you. All the better. The rules here is: *Every Fow uttered is a point made.* This is known as the Free-form Fow.

Variation Numero Four-o: This is the best part. When it finally gets to where everybody in the whole place is "Fowing" their guts out, you hand out Sony Walkmans to everbody on your Mixed Triples team. Make sure there's some Barbara Mandrell on there, maybe a little Conway Twitty, and, of course, some early Wayne Newton. You see the beauty here? Everbody else is making a jerk of themselves, yelling "Fow" at one another, and you're playing tennis. Pretty soon you'll be *Donka-Shaning* your opponent into oblivion. Game, set, and aerobic dancewear endorsement.

Course, here in America, we're normally not playing Mixed Triples. So I'm gonna give out a little free advice for the ordinary, normal mixed-doubles player, too. So at this time, please refer to diagram number one. We're going to learn something that I teach in my seniors classes, especially to the ones that are senile and forget how to actually play the game. It's called the Confused Identity Volley. Pay attention, cause I only wanna explain it once.

Let's say you're losing. Let's say you're down about, oh, three service breaks. Let's say you don't know what the heck to do, because the opposing team knows how to play better than you do. A lot of people give up at this point. They say, "I can't win this game, because the people on the other side of the net play better than me." But I want you to know and believe, right here and right now, that *it's not how well you play the game that counts, it's how well you bring the other guys down to your level.*

So here's what you do. It's 4–1 their way. Time to change ends of the court. You start to the right (see Figure 1), your partner to the left. But instead of going to the other side, your partner (B on the diagram) starts mumbling incoherently and walking directly toward the bench, flailing his racket wildly. Then, when he reaches point X on the diagram, he buries his face in a towel and explodes in barely muffled obscenities, ending with the following words:

". . . and looks exactly like Renée Richards."

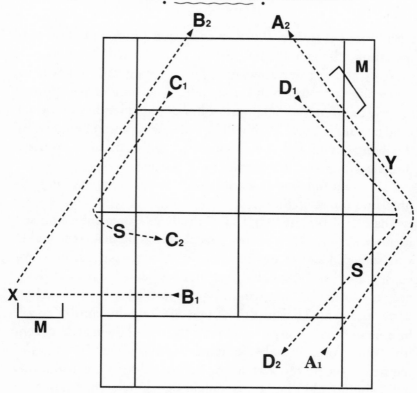

Figure 1: Diagram of tennis court to illustrate the Confused Identity Volley. Partners A and B, located at points A_1 and B_1, begin changing sides, with B following a somewhat erratic course toward point X, location of first obnoxious nonsensical remark. Remark should travel no farther than dotted line C_1-C_2, indicating the path of opponent C. When partner A reaches point Y, second obnoxious nonsensical remark should be uttered, this time traveling the length and breadth of the court, stopping C and D dead in their tracks at points S. Optional mumbling areas, to further confuse identities and direction of remarks, are indicated by brackets M.

If uttered correctly, these six words will carry only a few feet—just far enough to be heard by opponent C, who, at that moment, should be rounding the net en route to his or her position for the next game. Your partner should continue mumbling into the towel—any words will do, but I suggest obscure

Irish limericks to cause further confusion—but the only words that should be actually *audible* are the six listed above.

Now, at the same time that this is going on, you will be traversing the court to the other side. When you arrive approximately at point *Y*—make sure your opponent has had sufficient time to utter remark *X*—it will be time for your counter play. At this point say the following sentence, loudly and in its entirety, directing it cross-court toward your partner:

"That's nothing—you should of heard what happened in their hotel room last night."

That's it. You have now successfully executed the Confused Identity Volley. When properly used, opposing players C and D will sometimes stop dead in their tracks, perplexed, nervous, exasperated, and suspicious that they are being laughed at. They aren't, of course. That would be unsportsmanlike, to laugh at your opponent. They just think they are, and they probly won't be able to think of anything else for the rest of the match, except for: "*Who* looks exactly like Renée Richards?" and "What *did* happen in the hotel room last night, and whose hotel room was it?" I should add that, at no time in the entire recorded history of the Confused Identity Volley, has anyone ever *once* said, "What the heck yall talkin about?" If this ever did happen, however, the correct response is:

"Oh, I beg your pardon, I didn't realize I was speaking so loudly. Please excuse me. That was so rude. I'm so embarrassed. . . ." etc. Then keep apologizing about once every four games for the rest of the match, so that eventually they decide you were *definitely* talking about them. But that's another lesson, when you get into Advanced Identity Tennis. For the time being I'll just leave you with this tennis thought for the day:

Why won't Dick Van Patten go away?

I t's a horrible thing to behold when your best friend keels over on the sidewalk, grabs his stomach, and screams out, "Betty-Ford me! Betty-Ford me!" But, unfortunately, we live today in an addictive society where these scenes are all too common, especially at the corner of Elm and Akard in downtown Dallas. I'd advise you to avoid that area. It doesn't have to happen to you, though. You can save your friends from suddenly flopping around on their stomachs like headless gators, frothing at the mouth and screaming out Judas Priest lyrics. You can be *alert* to the telltale Signs of Addiction.

Have you or a loved one done any of the following things? If so, you might have a junkie in your house.

1. Your teenage daughter hasn't eaten solid food in three weeks, and she hasn't slept in six. She insists she's "just dieting and studying for a midterm."

2. Every time you pass a bar, your co-worker wants to stop in because "I love peanuts in a plastic bowl."

3. Your wife is convinced the elementary-school PTA has a contract out on her.

4. Six guys come up to you after church and say, "Will you be bringing your wife to any more parties?"

5. Your best friend tells you he has a computer program that's figured out what the point spread should be on the 1995 Super Bowl.

6. The same best friend asks you to loan him $74,000— "just till next Monday night."

7. When you take your secretary to Denny's, her only decision is whether to order the left side or the right side of the menu. Later, she orders the Nacho Plate "for the road."

8. A female co-worker orders *The Jim and Tammy Faye Bakker Story* to read on her coffee break, and starts talking about how "mean" you are because "I don't think Tammy looks that bad, when you see her in the right light."

9. Someone you dated three months ago calls to ask, "Did I leave my car over there?"

10. When the cop asks, "Do you know why I pulled you over?," you answer, "You're depressed and you need to talk to somebody."

11. When the cop asks, "Do you know why I pulled you over?," you answer, "So *you're* the one who pulled me over, huh?"

12. When the cop asks, "Do you know why I pulled you over?," you answer, "I'm pulled over?"

13. When the cop asks, "Do you know why I pulled you over?," you answer, "No, my radio only gets AM."

14. When the cop asks, "Do you know why I pulled you over?," you answer, "Does this count on the final?"

15. Your friend tells you he's licked his drinking problem because he figured out "It's that twelfth scotch that does it—I'm stopping at eleven tonight."

16. Later that night, the same friend says, "I know, I know—it's the twelfth one, but who said I can't get drunk once every day or so?"

17. One morning a co-worker says he's found a new drug that is absolutely nonaddictive. Later that day he tells you that some time during the night he lost his ability to operate a Coke machine.

18. A co-worker is reading this essay over your shoulder right now and laughing too hard.

19. A co-worker is reading this essay over your shoulder and saying, "I don't know what he means."

20. A co-worker is reading this essay over your shoulder and saying, "Hey, man, I been there."

ZOMBIE FILING

Acouple years ago this store called Bizmart opened down the street from my house. It's an office-supply store the size of Argentina. Eighteen-foot-high metal shelves full of Sticky Notes. Gross boxes of Flair pens. Thick forests of fluorescent desk lamps. Double-decker coffee makers for seventy people. It's kind of like going to a lumberyard in the slums, but without the glamour.

At first I thought it was a harmless addition to the neighborhood. After all, how many times in your life do you need to visit a store with five square miles of floor space because, "Oh, *shoot,* I forgot to pick up Liquid Paper this week"? It's not like anything in the store is a necessity of life.

Wrong.

People have been known to go in this place at nine in the morning and not come out for three days. I've lost five secretaries wandering around in there. About a year ago, I asked Wanda Bodine to help me tidy up around the office, set up a few file cabinets, and she said, "Okay, I'll stop by Bizmart on my way over," and—wham!—seven Bekins vans were backed up to my front door, unloading navy-blue monogrammed leatherette legal-pad holders.

"Wanda, what is this stuff?"

"What stuff?"

"Well, for example, what is this triple-decker computer-diskette storage file and tax-function calculator?"

"Oh, Joe Bob, they had so many *wonderful* things over there. You're going to be soooooooo *organized*."

"Wanda, I won't even need the tax-function calculator, because you just spent my income from now till 1997."

"Oh, Joe Bob, that reminds me. If you're planning on something in 1997, then you'll want to write it down in this Super Day Planner Report Binder."

"The one with Darryl Strawberry's picture on the front of it?"

"Those were *two dollars* cheaper than the others."

At first I wanted to chain Wanda up by her elbows and rub cat food in her face, but friends intervened and convinced me that Wanda didn't *mean* to spend $4,683 on office supplies in one afternoon. She couldn't *help* it. She had a disease. She was an Office Supply Zombie.

Later I found out what they were talking about. You can go into Bizmart at any time of the day or night, and people are wandering around, aisle to aisle, with glazed expressions on their faces. They're grazing! In an office-supply store! Maybe they went in there to buy a package of triplicate expense-account forms, but once they're inside, they say, "You know what? If I got one of these twenty-thousand-sheet boxes of nine-and-a-half by eleven computer paper, we'd save *fifty-seven percent* off retail!" And then somebody points out to em that they don't own a computer. So they buy a fifty-thousand-sheet box at 68 percent off retail.

It's hard to explain. Maybe it's the ventilation system. But you're wandering along, looking for mailing labels and ink pens, and suddenly you think, "Wow! Plastic magazine holders!," or "Wow! An Easy-Access Software Guide Wheel! It has every single computer command you could ever need on it!" And the problem is that you're alone. You're an addict and you're alone. You don't have a friend along to say, "Or you could just throw away the magazines when you're through with them."

And the longer you're in the place, the more the addiction builds. You start grazing over toward dangerous stuff, like Jumbo Business-Card Holders, brass-plated letter trays, and the Eldon Filing Tub (you hook it over the end of the file drawer to hold the stuff you're filing). Or, if you're really far gone, you start looking at stuff like the $300 Personal Document Shredder, fireproof filing safes, or the Commercial Business System High-Back Traditional Tilt-Swivel Leather Executive Chair. You start lusting after typewriters that have a 75,000-word built-in electronic dictionary, even though you don't know how to use an electronic dictionary, or, for that matter, a typewriter. You start thinking, "Wouldn't it be nice if everyone in the office had foot warmers?" You decide that all the "While You Were Out" telephone message pads are outdated and you need the new kind— the ones that have thirty-eight different boxes to check, including "Left a mildly disturbing threat" and "Deceased."

You are in the midst of what we have come to call, around my house, a Bizmart orgy. There is only one help for it. If you want to avoid entering your office every day and confronting a black Magic Marker board with orange writing on it (Wanda bought it one day when we weren't watching), then there's only one solution. We use the buddy system. Anyone entering Bizmart must be with a nonaddicted partner. The job of the partner is to say, "Maybe we'll come back tomorrow and get the map-of-the-world wall-size time clock. Go ahead, put it back on the shelf. In the next four or five days, I'll help you find out the correct time in Libya anytime you need it."

I just wish I knew what to do with the eighty-four gallon-size bottles of Toshiba copier fluid. Come to think of it, I saw this Toshiba copier last time I was in there. . . .

WHO'S PLAYING?

WHAT'S THE SCORE?

WHY ARE YOU WATCHING THIS STUFF?

There's a certain season when, no matter what time of the day or night it is, you can turn on cable TV and watch the Duke Blue Devils play the UNLV Runnin Rebels in the Carrier Dome. Or maybe I'm mixed up here—*that's* not the game I watched three hours ago, it was ... uh ... the Villanova Wildcats in the Saluki Winter Classic against De Paul. But that doesn't make sense. No, it was the Oregon Ducks in the Saluki Winter Classic, but *somebody* played De Paul. Maybe that was the Atlantic Coast–Big East Challenge Classic. What are Salukis anyway? Or was it the Oregon Beavers? They're not the Ducks, they're the Beavers. No, it's the Oregon *State* Beavers, and they weren't in the Saluki Classic. They were in the Bob's Big Boy Classic at the University of Hawaii.

Anyhow, I can't remember exactly which games I've been watching, but I *loved* every single one of them.

Women don't understand this. Women come in the room while you're watching the game, and they say, "Who's winning?"

No woman has ever cared who's winning. They ask this question to bait us.

So you answer em. "Alabama-Birmingham."

"What?"

"Alabama-Birmingham. The University of Alabama at Birmingham."

"I didn't know it was in Birmingham."

By now you've missed a twenty-eight-foot three-pointer because you're trying to explain where the goldurn school is.

"They call it UAB. Because the main university is in Tuscaloosa."

"Who are they playing?"

She doesn't care about this either.

"Miami of Florida."

"I think everybody *knows* where Miami is."

Patience. Patience. "It's because there's *another* University of Miami, but it's in Ohio."

Meanwhile, a hotshot guard has run a fast break the length of the court, passed off to a six-ten forward, who slam-dunked the ball, got fouled, and made the UAB coach so mad he's about to get a technical for yelling at the referee.

"Watch this. They're gonna throw him out."

So then we sit there for a minute, watching the coach windmill his arms down the court, screaming at the top of his lungs.

He rips off his jacket and throws it down on the court, stomps on it, and continues to scream.

She says, "They get so upset, don't they?"

And then after a while, she'll say, "Why are you watching a team in Alabama and a team in Florida? Do you know anything about those schools?"

See, this is the point where, no matter what the man says, the woman will never understand. Because she's right. Five minutes before the game started, I could have cared less whether UAB and Miami had basketball teams or not, who won this game, or, for that matter, whether they even *played* this game.

So what happened?

Here's the best way I can explain it. I started flipping the cable-TV remote control, walking that little baby all the way around the dial, and when it hit ESPN—wham!—there were eighteen thousand people in an arena somewhere screaming at the top of their lungs. Passion! They *care* about this stuff! It's *real*! And so you sort of get sucked in. You say, "Maybe I'll keep this on just long enough to see what game this is, where they're playing."

And then while you're waiting for ESPN to put the score up, so you can see what the two teams are, the announcer says something about Rodney Smith, the six-four guard for Seton Hall, and Fritz Weirichs, the seven-foot-two German center for Syracuse, being two of the outstanding players in the country. I've never watched a game yet on ESPN where they didn't have at least one of "the most outstanding pure athletes I've ever watched play the game." And so you watch this guy for a while. You wanna see him dunk the ball or hit a three-pointer or block a shot or something.

And then one of three things happens:

1. The guy gets fouled and the referee is *blind*. He doesn't see the foul. The play goes on. Some guy steals the ball from him and lays it in. He was *robbed*, but the referee was so *stupid* . . . blah blah blah . . . In other words, suddenly, you're *steamed*. You saw the instant replay. It was an *injustice*.

2. Or, the guy makes a great play, blocks a shot, but the referee blows the whistle and calls a foul on him anyway. Another injustice.

3. Or, the crowd is so mean that they start booing the opposing team, throwing objects onto the court, taunting the players every time they throw the ball out of bounds. A surly crowd means . . . the members of the visiting team are becoming *martyrs* in our eyes. In other words, it's not fair. It's another injustice.

Now. Once you have *witnessed* an injustice—any injustice—you *must* keep watching the game. The martyred visiting team *must* triumph over the surly crowd. The guard who was robbed will prove the referee wrong. The guy who blocked the shot will get his revenge.

So the answer to the question—"Why are you watching this game?"—is an easy one:

The game is just like life. Only, when you get shafted, you don't have to spend three years suing somebody, or whining about it, or asking some government agency to fix it. The game goes on *immediately*. You have a chance to *win*. You have a chance to make somebody else *lose*. You have a chance, at the end of the game, when you're up by five points and there's only twenty-seven seconds left, to win the game simply by being *smarter* than the other person—simply by *refusing to play*. You just successfully bounce the ball for twenty-seven seconds. This is sooooooo satisfying.

"Why are you still watching? They're just gonna bounce the ball for twenty-seven seconds and then it will be over. They've already won the game."

You gals just go stick in some aerobics tapes till we're finished, okay? It's too hard to explain.

I can't get Jessica Hahn out of my mind. I'm trying. I keep saying to myself, "Well, okay, that's
it, she's gone, she's history, we won't be hearing about her
again." And then here she comes again, hiking up her dress,
scrunching her bazoomas together, prancing her stiletto high
heels through the media like an ad for the world's longest-
running makeover.

Somebody sent me an ad from the El Lay *Times* with a
bleached-out picture of Jessica wearing an eight-inch-long
pointy earring, forty-seven pounds of frizzed hair, and an expression on her face that says, "Where did I leave that nail
polish?"

The ad is for the "30th (Diamond Anniversary) Exotic Car Show" at the Long Beach Convention Center, and under Jessica's picture it says, "MEET JESSICA HAHN—possibly her last California Live Appearance—Don't Miss It!"

People all over Long Beach were saying, "Now, Herb, we missed Jessica the last two times she was in town. If you don't get tickets for this car show, we may never be able to see her. This is her farewell tour."

Then, the next thing I know, Jessica is in Columbus, Ohio, doing a radio promotion called "Spend the Morning in Bed with Jessica Hahn." The radio station put a big bed in the studio, and the lucky prize-winner *crawled under the sheets with her.* Then the general manager, program director, and a couple of deejays posed for a picture, *in bed with Jessica,* covers pulled up under their chins, with painful grins on their faces, like bankers undergoing hiney surgery.

Okay, let's stop here a minute and review. I'm gonna try to fit all this together.

First, Jessica, we had the Jim Bakker thing. We tried to feel sorry for you, because, after all, that's like getting sexually molested by Daffy Duck. And anyway, you were young, you were impressionable, you sort of had a crush on this preacher guy who put you up to it. But, honey, your solution to the deal was to get *money* out of Jimbo. Bad choice, Jess.

But we forgave you for that, because there was this lathered-up lawyer with you, and he was influencing everything you did.

Okay, next item. "I don't wanna talk about it." No interviews. But you would *sell* the story to Hugh Hefner.

Okay okay okay okay okay, no big deal. Everybody has the right to make a buck. Your story, your rules.

And then there was the plastic-surgery deal. Oh, all right.

Everybody's doing it. You probly thought you were ugly or something.

And then you live at the Playboy Mansion for a while. And then, when the magazine comes out, it's not just your story, it's this full-frontal Lady Godiva deal. And by the way, Jessica, *excellent* plastic surgeon. Very impressive. "I'm doing this for me," you told everybody. Okay okay okay okay. It's the eighties.

And then you go on all the talk shows, and everybody is so *mean* to you. I admit it, Jessica, they were kinda cruel, the way they talked to you. And you sat there like a whipped weenie dog, wondering whether your mascara would hold up, and so that didn't work out too well, did it?

And then there was the Sam Kinison video, where you wallowed around like a pig and showed a lot of thigh. Great video, but then Sam goes on the radio and tells everybody that a) he had sex with you, and b) you were . . . how do I say this? . . . you were not exactly *satisfactory*.

And so you're at the Exotic Car Show.

And so you're in a fake bed at the Columbus radio station.

Now. Jessica. Before your life becomes a really bad fifties movie, can I offer a little advice?

Number one, everybody thinks they're ugly. It's kind of the shared mental disease of the twentieth century. The ones that have plastic surgery *still* think they're ugly most of the time.

Number two, there's a pattern here. The pattern is that, every time you get offered something—either sex or money or fame or religion—you think it's gonna change your life. Honey, the world is full of offers. They don't ever change your life.

Number three, you seem to need money. Sleazeballs notice this and tell you how to get money.

Jessica, they're just sleazeballs. The preacher, the lawyer, Reverend Jimbo, Sam Kinison. They're just sleazeballs, hon.

They were always sleazeballs.

Okay, go ahead. That's all I got to say. Remember: "Sleazeballs."

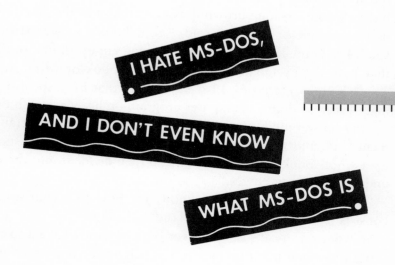

I HATE MS-DOS, AND I DON'T EVEN KNOW WHAT MS-DOS IS

I was talking on the phone last week to Brad and Trudy Brinker, the most up-to-date couple I know. Of course, I had to make an appointment to talk to Brad and Trudy. They have a talking recorder-hoojie on their phone that makes appointments for messages, stock transfers, or actual talking. Actual talking is discouraged, though, because Brad and Trudy Brinker are involved with living their wonderful lives. Also, while I'm on the subject, you should never call Brad and Trudy between eight-thirty and nine at night, because that's their "nurturing time." I'm not exactly sure what they do, but I assume they force each other to sit in the same room together for a whole half hour.

Anyhow, I was calling up Brad and Trudy because they wrote me this note on "Brad and Trudy" stationery with New Mexico Indian women in long brown dresses staring into the desert all down one side of it, and it said, "Your book was wonderful, Ciao, Brad and Trudy." And I was calling em up to find out if they read the Eyetalian translation of my book or what. And Trudy had an interesting answer. She said that Brad spent one night last year doing a computer program on his Macintosh PC 67,000-bit, 24-million-ram 10-K Form 1040 Home Entertainment Unit, and what he did is, he taught the computer to suck up a whole book, read it for him, and then divide it into three-and-a-half-minute "bytes."

"You may be interested to know, Joe Bob, that your book consists of seventy-four bytes," Trudy told me.

So what this means is, whenever Brad or Trudy have a spare three-and-a-half minutes, they just punch up the book on their screen, and they read it for three-and-a-half minutes, and then they punch a key, and it tells the computer to hold it right there for em, till the next time some leisure downtime opens up in their lives.

"Wouldn't it be easier," I asked her, "to use a bookmark?"

At this point Brad came on the phone—evidently he had a little time off from exercising his $10,000 Russian wolfhound—and he said, "The computer can actually organize leisure time more efficiently than you or I could. Once you read past the three-and-a-half-minute threshold, you start to repeat sentences. Viacom International, the company that owns MTV, has spent a lot of research money on this. Your reading-efficiency quotient takes a dramatic tumble at the 210-second point."

"Wouldn't some people be different?" I said. "Like wouldn't a Tolstoy reader be different from a Tama Janowitz reader? Course, I guess that's the point you're making. You don't really have to know how to *read* to enjoy Tama Janowitz. You can just watch the publicity tour."

"You could be right about other cultures," said Brad. "I'll schedule that for investigation. But I know that for *this* culture, the three-and-a-half-minute reading byte is exactly the right length."

"You mean for Americans?"

"No no no. America is multicultural, Joe Bob. I mean the Brad-and-Trudy-Brinker culture, our own environment as defined by our upbringing and awareness. Got to go, Joe Bob, we're networking tonight."

And then a little later Trudy had to leave, too, so she could go to a workshop where she was planning to open up her personal prosperity through tapping the inner, unconscious screenplays that are being automatically written by her producer/director self. But before she got off the phone, I asked her one last question.

"Trudy, what if you put a book in your computer and you don't *like* the book, and then you've got all these three-and-a-half-minute bytes to read? What would you do?"

"Oh, we never start things we don't finish."

"You don't? You'd read the book, no matter how bad it was?"

"Joe Bob, 'bad' is a negative-force word. We don't believe there are 'good' and 'bad,' only fulfilling and draining."

"Well, in that case, was my book fulfilling or draining?"

"*Very* fulfilling, Joe Bob. We got many usable ideas from it."

"There really weren't any usable ideas *in* it."

"It was the energy, though. We felt the energy, we used it, and we improved ourselves with it."

And it was at that moment that I knew my life as a writer was over.

I BURNED THE FLAG (I THINK)

My nominees for this year's Dueling Dimwits are the people who are burning up the flag, and the people who are *beating up* the people who are burning up the flag. I think anybody who actually takes the time to get lathered up on *either* side of this issue should be taxed a hundred bucks a year just for the hassle it's gonna cause the cops on the street. You think it's such a *big deal* they're burning the flag, *you* go out there and haul em off to jail by the scruff of their necks. These people are gonna be the hardest people to arrest since the Fetus Fans.

"But, Joe Bob, it's a *civil-liberties* issue! You can't just let . . ."

Okay okay okay okay okay. Be quiet. Let's look at it like

reasonable human beans. Let's start with the Betsy Ross Haters:

"I have a right to burn the flag as an expression of free speech."

Yes, you do. As a matter of fact, when I was in the Boy Scouts color guard, they told us if we ever *screwed up* and let the flag drag across the ground at the Arkansas Razorbacks football game, then we'd have to take it home and you guessed it . . . *burn* it!

I don't think we're gonna send out the National Guard to arrest the den mothers who sanction Cub Scout flag burnings, are we? As you probly know, the Cub Scouts are the *worst*. Sometimes they drag the flag around on the ground *just to see if it's true*. But normally the den mothers say, "Oh, no, I guess we'll have to burn that flag," and then they *secretly* wash it. Den mothers have been doing this for years, unaware that they were being excessively patriotic.

Nope, it's not the Scouts they're gonna go after. And you know why? Because the Scouts have a *good reason* to burn the flag.

And do you know what happens when we start asking federal judges to decide who has a *good reason* to do something and who has a *bad reason* to do something?

I thought so.

"But, Joe Bob, my daddy and my granddaddy fought and died for that flag. And if we ever have another war . . ."

Okay okay okay okay okay. Shut up. First of all, you *will not*. And they *did not*. I don't recall that President Roosevelt went on the radio and said, "My fellow Americans, I have grave news. At exactly 8:02 this morning, the Japanese government launched an unprovoked attack against our military base in

Pearl Harbor, Hawaii. During the first hour of combat, several hundred people were killed and several ships destroyed. But at 9:09, one of the Japanese bombs *destroyed one of our flags!* I'm afraid this means war." I don't remember it that way, do you?

I don't remember anybody coming home from Vietnam and saying, "Well, Son, Old Glory still flies. They kicked our hineys, but the *flag*, that's what *we* were fighting for."

So, please, don't go beating up people that don't have any more sense than to think the *flag* is what America is about. I think you can get one from a 1-800 number on TV. It's not like it's that big a deal.

And as to you people that are interested in burning it, or wearing flags on your hind end like Jimi Hendrix, I have an idea. I'm gonna start manufacturing a flag with *fifty-one* stars on it. You see the beauty here? You can burn this one all day long, because it's not *really* an American flag. It looks like one, until you get up real close and *count* the stars. You could get a thousand people up there on the Capitol steps and start burning up flags, and before you could get arrested, all the cops would have to *count the stars* on each flag. You'd have em all burned up before the cops got through. And the cops would like it, too. All they'd have to do is go get on the radio and say, "Well, Chief, we couldn't make any arrests. Lack of evidence. They might have burned some flags and they might not have. They might have just burned some cloth that *looked like* flags."

I think this would be much more fun, don't you?

Then the cops could go home and yall could beat *each other* up. Isn't that what you really want?

FAT, INCORPORATED

Are you fat? Do you resemble a pregnant Holstein that's been left on the feedlot for eight months? Do people stop you on the street and say, "Oh, excuse me, I thought you were my car"? Have there been times when you felt like giving up and simply applying for your own zip code?

Don't *worry* about it. Do you have nine hundred bucks? Great! The chance to strip away those unsightly flab lines within weeks, months, years, or certainly within the decade is within your reach. Do you have a Visa card? Even better! Join the millions who are doing the same thing you're doing—sitting around thinking about how *fat* they are.

Here are just a few of the programs you can choose from:
1. The Purdue University Total-Immersion Diet and Fitness Center: This six-month program begins with a big surprise—you can eat as much as you want! What's the catch? Patients are organized into "herds" and fenced off from other "herds" with "barbed-wire fence." This means that if you check in in September and you don't watch yourself, you'll chew off all the "good stuff" by October. Unless your medical supervisor pitches a little hay over the fence, you're going to be one lean individual. Then, when you're switched into a new pasture after three months, boy, will you welcome the change! A bonus: Twice a month you'll be dipped for ticks and checked for brucellosis. The trick, of course, is keeping that weight off after you return to "the city." Trained counselors from the Purdue Botany Department can help with a special high-soybean scientific maintenance diet. Wait until you see the "marbling effect" between your muscles. Cost: $500 per week, plus feed and veterinarian costs.
2. The Lucinda Willoughby "Beautiful Person Inside" Women's Therapy Diet: This is a group of incredibly fat housewives with husbands who are insurance adjusters and who meet three times a week in a suburban home in Provo, Utah, to try out new recipes like Lobster Newburg without lobster and Steak Diane without steak or, for that matter, Diane. After the women dine on their Chicken Enchilada "You Skinny Girl, You" Low-Sodium Cacciatore, they sing songs, tell stories, and agree to be mean to all the slender, pretty twenty-three-year-old wives in town. Results can be dramatic. Sue (Mrs. Carl) Brinson, who joined Lucinda Willoughby just six months

ago, has already dropped six pounds and is considered a bitch. Cost: $75 per week.

3. Opti-Nutri-Slim-Bender: This is a series of prepackaged dieter's meals that will fit into any 289-cubic-foot walk-in commercial freezer. Got a craving this morning for, say, eggs Benedict? Just go into your freezer, look under *E*, break open the silver foil package, mix with low-fat milk in a blender, and *drink* your eggs Benedict. Surprise! It tastes like a milk shake, doesn't it? Wait till you tell your friends you had an eggs Benedict–flavored milk shake. Or how about the middle of the night, when you feel like you'll die if you don't have a triple-decker salami-and-Swiss snack. Back to the freezer, this time under *S*. Yes, that's right! It's a salami-flavored milk shake! Who needs to diet when you can just drink milk shakes all the time? One word of caution: If you feel a craving for an actual milk shake, you can pick the Opti-Nutri-Slim-Bender *M*-pack, but it will taste like a liverwurst-and-macaroni casserole. Science hasn't worked out how to get that actual milk-shake taste yet. Cost: $12,000 per freezer-load (milk not included).

And, finally, for those who can't shuck the pounds any other way . . .

4. Camp Fatty, Alexandria, Va.: As soon as you arrive at the gates of Porker Academy, as it's known by the staff, you'll be issued a pig nose and a set of padded pork feet. You will be addressed only as "Hey, Beef Critter!" and will be expected to answer, "Yes, sir, Mr. Slim Person, sir!" Twice a day the public will be admitted for a demonstration of Porkchop Downs, in which all the inmates at Camp Fatty are released from a starting gate so they can race toward a coveted barbecue turkey leg. (Interested specta-

tors should inquire about group rates at the Washington, D.C., National Visitors Center. Simply say, "We wanna see them fat people rasslin over a turkey leg," and they'll know what you mean.) Anyone who doesn't lose at least one pound a day will be sent to Military Medical Post, where the required pound will be surgically shaved from the appropriate buttock. One thing you can say about this program. It works! People that went through the program ten years ago have lost up to five hundred pounds and *kept it off.* One happy student now weighs twenty-four pounds and lives exclusively on bamboo shoots. Cost: $17,500 per week.

5. Isn't it about time *you* started making yourself feel guilty again?

T he guys that run the Miss Texas USA Pageant and the Miss California USA Pageant have come out publicly against Hooker Wear. Without coming right out and saying it, they said, "We're changing our dress code so the girls don't look like hookers."

Now what was interesting about this is, it happened the exact same week that Jerry "I Own the Goldang Team" Jones of the Dallas Cowboys was telling the Dallas Cowboys Cheerleaders that they should look *more* like hookers. Then, after fourteen of em quit, he said it was all *just a misunderstanding* and he didn't really mean that they should wear bicycle pants and halter tops, and serve as hostesses at parties for Jerry's friends, and do beer commercials, and start giving him a percentage of what they make doing speeches. He said it might have *sounded* like he was asking for all those things, but what he really said was, "You gals are purty."

What we have here is a growing national trend, the product of every wife who has ever spent the car ride home from the party going on about "that *woman*"—you know the one . . . in the rhinestones, the leather, the sarong-wrap mini, the stiletto high heels, and the dangly Century 21 Real Estate earrings. Usually, this is *not* the twenty-year-old Hollywood starlet who was at the party. The starlet was probly wearing blue jeans and an Angora sweater. This was *Herb's wife!* That's what makes em so mad. There are just *so many* women who want to dress up like hookers you can't keep track of the real hookers anymore. Breast-enlargement surgery only costs $1,800, so women put it on *MasterCard!* And so now the women who hate Hooker Wear—and, by extension, all the organizations that these women control through their husbands—are the new American Hooker Police.

Here's the question we, as a nation, need to be asking ourselves: "Is she dressed like a hooker, or is she just trendy?"

Let's examine the evidence.

Richard Guy, producer of the Miss USA Pageants in Texas and California, told the *Dallas Morning News*, "Only *unclassy* women wear high heels and rhinestone earrings with swimsuits these days. Beauty pageants are for nice girls. Covering up is sexy. Showing everything is awful and cheap."

All right, I know a little bit about hookers. So let's see now, where do you find hookers wearing high heels and swimsuits?

Hollywood Boulevard? Nope. They favor miniskirts with puffy blouses that cover up *everything*.

Times Square? Nope. They tend to dress like Tina Turner, and not even the most rabid female in the Hooker Police would call Tina a hooker. Women love Tina, six-inch heels and all.

Harry Hines Boulevard? (For those of you from out-of-state, Harry Hines is a street in Dallas that's so rough we've got Hereford cattle out there turning tricks.) But no, the ladies of Harry Hines Boulevard wear tight blue jeans, loose-fitting tops, and outrageous wigs.

Laredo? No way, José. The most notorious hookers in Boys Town wear colorful party dresses.

Mustang Ranch, Nevada? Dressed to the nines.

So where are these women who wear high heels and swimsuits—these women that are not "nice girls"?

They're in beauty pageants! That's the *only* place women have *ever* worn swimsuits and heels. In fact, hookers have *more* modesty than the beauty queens. And now that I'm on this subject, come to think of it, hookers abandoned hot pants ten years ago. So who wears hot pants?

It's the Dallas Cowboys Cheerleaders that still wear hot pants! The ones that insist on their moral purity!

So what's going on here? Why, suddenly, would these guys at the Miss USA Pageant decide they needed to hire Esther Williams to design new swimsuits for the girls? She did, too—the same kind she used to wear in the movies, the kind that made her look like an East German shot-putter. And when they had the Texas pageant this week, there they all were, trussed up in Hawaiian-style super-bras and nine yards of material stretched straight across their hips, and they were prancing around barefoot. In other words, they did their best to make all the girls look like . . . well . . . like your sister.

And did they look like hookers?

Nope. They looked like women that had spent seventeen thousand hours on the Nautilus equipment getting their midriffs down to nothing and their calves toned up—so that they could then *cover up* their midriffs and let their calves sink back down to earth as they tried to prance on the balls of their feet. They looked like women who were ashamed of their bodies.

Of course, they *weren't* ashamed of their bodies.

It was the Miss USA guys who were ashamed of their bodies.

That's okay with me—they can make up whatever rules they want to make up—but they ought to stop talking about it. They're giving hookers a bad name.

My MasterCard bill came in with $367 worth of charges from the Love Line 900 number, and I'm furious. There's so many irresponsible people in this world, they can't even keep simple phone records correctly. I know I didn't spend more than $250, $260 last month on the Love Line.

Actually, it wouldn't have been that high, but I met this professional model named Bunny Ragsdale who's been on 347 magazine covers around the world and lives in Bozeman, Montana, and we spent about eight hours one night planning how I was gonna take over the management of her career now that she gets the top modeling money. Bunny can spend eight hours in front of a camera and take home money in the forty-, fifty-dollar range. Three years ago she was on the cover of the Swedish *Elle*. This month she's doing a calendar for Crenshaw's Auto Body. So she's keeping busy. Unfortunately, Bunny evidently changed her phone number the day after we talked and forgot to tell me. Bunny! Are you listening? I'm working on a cable deal!

It's amazing how many professional models with thirty-six-inch bust lines you can meet on the Love Line. What you do is, you call up and listen to a bunch of recordings that go like this:

"Hi, I'm the Octopus Lady and I'm lonely. I currently live in the San Diego area, but could relocate for the right financial arrangement. I love oldies bands, like the Ramones. I have two gorgeous dimples and red red hair. I'm so embarrassed doing this. I wish someone would *call* me."

And then if you wanna leave a message for the Octopus Lady, you press a button on your phone, or if you don't, you can go right on to the next message until you find one you like. One problem, though—I'm warning you about this in case you're ready to try out the Love Line—is that you've got to be real careful about exactly which button you press. One night I punched a 3 instead of a 2 and left this long message describing my chest hairs for a guy named San Francisco Slave Boy. I'm *still* getting calls from that guy. Another time, I was trying to get through to the famous Love Line regular "Spanking Coed" in Bellevue, Illinois, but instead I made contact with "Smurf Master" in Saginaw, Michigan. He turned out to be a professional tractor-pull mechanic.

No, if you really wanna get some results from the Love Line, you've got to make up your own recording to put on there. And let's face it, this is the wave of the nineties. Newspaper ads are going downhill. I haven't changed my personal ad in the newspaper since 1987—you've seen it, I'm sure: "Musky Writer

Seeks Nookie." But I only get about three responses a year from it, and all of those are from women who have "height in proportion to weight." And we all know what *that* means: six-foot-eight, 390 pounds.

So if you're dialing around through the Love Line tonight, you just might find this message waiting:

"Yo! Why won't you go out with me? Lots of girls would *love* to go out with me, so why won't you? Huh? Oh, is something *wrong* with me? I guess you want some *sensitive* guy, don't you, some Cotton Docker Goonie with an Epson Computer growing out of his hip? Oh, I see, well, you're probly ugly anyway. Will you go out with me?"

I put this baby on there last night to try to get Tight Black Leather of Mesa, Arizona, to call me. Either her or Candy Witherspoon of Bangor, Maine. I think I could move to Maine, even with the winters and everything. I really could. I'm thinking about it.

Oh, and one more thing—don't even *think* about it, Dominant Slime Sweeper of Frankfort, Kentucky. I will *not* be taking your call.

FREQUENT FLYING

I'd rather not know exactly how many Frequent Flyer miles you have, thank you very much. This is nothing personal. In fact, I think it's wonderful that you qualified for triple miles on Delta and American, scored some Avis upgrades, and now you have enough miles to fly round-trip business class to Canberra, Australia, on Qantas. What I'm worried about is, when is everybody gonna start *using* these trips to Canberra? So far I've met 368 people with Frequent Flyer mileage in the six figures, and only one person who's actually cashed in. (That guy, by the way, used the miles to fly his family from Dallas to Miami, and he *already* regretted it. After all, he was already 25 percent of the way to Athens, and he *wasted* his miles on a domestic flight.)

Why has the whole country turned into a bunch of nerds

because of a few free handouts? I'm gonna start asking people that sit next to me in airplanes to discuss the MS-DOS computer language on an IBM-compatible PC. It's a much *sexier* conversation than this:

"This is a 1,342-miler. I make it twice a month."

"Wow! You must be racking up some Frequent Flyer miles!"

"Me and the wife are going for the five-hundred-thousand-mile Bangkok–Hong Kong–Helsinki package on JAL."

"I think I've heard about that one. Does it include the donkey act in Helsinki?"

"We have no idea. But we just thought, what the hell, *free flying*, might as well take it."

"Otherwise you never would have seen Helsinki."

"Nope. Or, we could fly to Vegas and back twenty-seven times. But the wife told me she doesn't want to do that."

"That would be fun, too."

You guys realize what's gonna happen, don't you? The airlines are putting cutoff dates on Frequent Flyers now, like "Use em in three years or lose em." This means that three years from now, *all* of us will be going to Canberra, Australia, at the same time! But that's not even the worst part.

The worst part is that *none* of us will want to be there. We'll all be over there wandering around among the sagebrush staring at the same koala bears and saying, "Nah, see, I *had* to come. I had too many Frequent Flyers *not* to come."

Didn't we already learn this lesson with S&H Green Stamps in the fifties and sixties? Remember those? For a long time it seemed like a great idea to go to the grocery store, leave with a basket of food and a ten-foot strip of stamps, stay up all night pasting them in a book so Mom could get a free toaster and Dad could have that baby-blue windbreaker he was always wanting.

And then one day everyone just quit collecting Green Stamps.

It might have been the day the discount grocery down the street opened up—the one that didn't give away stamps but *did* have prices that were a nickel lower on coffee and canned asparagus. Or maybe it was the day Dad took a big trash can full of broken electric can openers, bent toy wagons, and ripped T-shirts that said KICK ME on the back, out to the Dempster Dumpster.

"What if we didn't go to the Green Stamp store anymore?" Dad said.

And Mom said, "Thank goodness I don't have to figure *that* out anymore."

You can just take it out of the price of my airplane ticket, if you would, *por favor.*

BEADS OF OCEAN SPRAY, GLISTENING ON CHRISTIE BRINKLEY'S BREASTS

I t took me three weeks to finally finish reading the *Sports Illustrated* Twenty-Fifth Anniversary Glistening-Beads-of-Ocean-Spray Issue, but it was because I was taking notes on every article. Since there have only been about 39 million words written about this particular issue, I'm sure we have unanswered questions that only I would bother to ask.

Unanswered Question Numero Uno: How do they get Spandex Lycra to do that little flip between their breasts, like a skinny cruller donut?

Numero Two-o: How come every single one of the *Sports Illustrated* swimsuit models was ugly as a three-ton dump truck in the eighth grade, but then "one day this man asked me to model and I was flabbergasted"? What is God telling us here?

Numero Three-o: When you're in the eighth grade, should you find the ugliest girl in your class and ask her out and then get engaged to her by the time you're sixteen, right before some man asks her to model? Does this mean when she's twenty-two she'll have a body that will make grown men keel over, pant for air, and beg for mercy? Should we ask somebody in the eighth grade to test this out for us?

Numero Four-o: What about the girl who was so beautiful in the eighth grade she would never talk to you? Is she a bag lady today? Do dogs run away from her? This would be a nice thing that God has done, if it's true.

Numero Five-o: If these are really the most beautiful women in the world, why do they have to go to Cancun for three months and take ninety-seven thousand exposures of film in order to get one decent picture in a swimsuit?

Numero Six-o: Once they *know* they're one of the most beautiful women in the world—in other words, once "this man" asks em to model and they're flabbergasted and then they make millions doing it—why do they decide to wear baggy army pants and tie their hair up behind their ears and put on a floppy sweatshirt and go down to the local fruit market to squeeze tangerines and prove that "nobody ever notices me on the street"? Why is this important? Why do they all talk about it, like they wanna prove how ugly they are? What is God trying to show us here?

Numero Seven-o: Why, when the reporter comes to interview them, are they always doing something like laying bathroom tile in their beach house? Don't they know he's coming for the interview?

Numero Eight-o: When the reporter knocks on their door, why do they open the door with a trowel and a bucket of paint in their hands and say, "Real glamorous, isn't it"? Why do they want us to know that they're *not* glamorous? Isn't that the whole point of being a model, to be glamorous? Do they mean this? If they mean it, why do they do it (model, that is)? If they don't mean it, why do they say it?

Numero Nine-o: Why do they retire from modeling in 1972, and then retire again from modeling in 1974, and then retire again from modeling in 1980, and now they're really retiring from modeling, except they're doing thirty shoots this year for "a good friend of mine, a wonderful man I've worked with for years"? If they're models, why do they have to "retire" at all? They don't get any Social Security, do they? Why can't they just say, "I don't want to do that this month, but maybe next month"? Is this too hard to understand?

Numero Ten-o: Why do they hate makeup? This one really should be the *easiest* to understand. If they hate makeup, then they ought to have some reason, like "It irritates my eyes," or "It makes my skin look like cheap Tupperware from the Goodwill store." But instead of that, they just say, "I hate to put on this stuff"—*while they're putting it on.*

In other words, after twenty-five years of *Sports Illustrated*'s Jiggle-rama, I still don't know exactly what God is trying to show us here. I think I'll go back and study it some more.

TAKE MY DESSERT, PLEASE

When did dessert become so hysterically funny? Something happened in the last five years, right? They slipped something into the dessert and they didn't tell me. Is this what happened? Come on, you guys—what's in it? Tell me.

Why is it that every time I go to a restaurant, the waiter comes sniveling up to the table like a guy in a Cheech and Chong movie. "You guys need some *stuff*, man?" No, what he really says is, "You aren't going to *believe* what we have on the dessert cart tonight." Giggle giggle wink wink. "We have kiwi tarts, a crème caramel, and I would suggest [here he sighs so loudly you think somebody just deflated a balloon in the Macy's Parade] the

Bailey's Irish Cream cheesecake. If you haven't had it, you'll want to stuff parts of it in your underwear and *wear* it home."

Ha ha ha. Funny funny funny. But here's the interesting part. Up to now the guy's just a dim-bulb character who likes to dress up in a sailor suit and spoon crème broolay out of a bowl for a living. But then *everybody at the table joins in.* We are now into the stand-up-comedy part of the meal, and we won't be out of it for another fifteen minutes.

"I can't believe you would do this to us," says Shirley the 450-pound mustachioed woman. (It's always the fat person who speaks first.) "You're so *naughty.*"

Ha ha. Giggle giggle.

"I really shouldn't," says Harvey. "What did you say was in that triple-chocolate sack of strawberries and cream in a raspberry purée with chocolate ice cream? Besides the chocolate, of course."

I usually try to break up this riotous laugh fest by saying something to the guy like "Nothing."

Now the word "nothing" is a good word. It's definite. It's simple. It means exactly what it says. And you would think it would be final, wouldn't you?

Not to the Dim Bulb. The Dim Bulb says, "Nothing? Are you sure? Not even a little flan? How about one of our peach tarts?"

What am I supposed to do? Beat him up? Demand to see his waiter ID? Give him proof that my hearing is intact?

Nope. Can't do anything. You know why? It's now *his* table. Everybody's on *his* side.

"Come on, Joe Bob, have some of my baked Alaska. I'll order it if you'll help me."

"I don't want to *help you* eat a baked Alaska. If I wanted to help you, I would buy you an Abdomenizer. If I wanted to eat a baked Alaska, I would order a baked Alaska. But I don't have any interest in helping *you* eat *your* baked Alaska."

Now you may be wondering why I've got to take such a hard line on this issue, why I've got to turn outright hostile to get these people to shut up. And it's because they don't *believe* me. They're all convinced that somewhere in my gut I'm crying out to stuff three, four baked Alaskas down my throat, maybe wash it down with some Peach Melba Triple-Hoss Napoleons or something. They *know* this has to be true. They've figured it out. They're certain. So, finally, they give up on me and they turn to the other people at the table.

"Why don't we just get two and share?"

"Should we get the Bananas Foster?"

Ha ha ha. Guffaw guffaw. I've never delivered a punch line that gets the laugh this punch line gets. "Should we get the Bananas Foster?" Bob Hope would pay $5,000 for this punch line, based on the reaction it will get at whatever dinner table I happen to be sitting at.

"How about one torte and one chocolate mousse?"

"All right," says Shirley the warthog. "You talked me into it."

Laugh laugh. Guffaw guffaw. Because, you see, nobody talked Shirley into it. It was Shirley's idea in the first place.

"Should I bring five spoons?" This is Mr. Dim Bulb's attempt to get me back into this group-therapy session.

"Nothing," I say to him. "No torte. No mousse. No chocolate double-reverse flan flipper. No dessert. *Nada*. Nothing."

"Ahhhhhhhh, Joe Bob . . ." And the whole thing starts all over again.

And then they bring the stuff, and everybody spears it with these tiny little forks off of everybody else's plate, and then they comment on every single bite of it—"This is so sinful."

"This is better than sex." "I'm gonna feel soooooo guilty to-morrow."

Let me point something out to you people:

Food is not sinful.

Food is not better than sex.

Food is not something you talk about. It's something you *eat*.

Food is food.

Unless . . . Come on, you guys, tell me. What *are* they putting in the dessert? Really?

DAD'S CASKET

I buried my dad in Little Rock one week ago as I write this. And since he was one of the world's greatest bargain shoppers ("Son, I know a place downtown in the furniture district where you can get that *exact same suit* for twenty-five dollars"), I figured he would appreciate my spending a little time on the casket selection.

Of course, I was planning to get whichever casket Mama wanted. I knew this, the undertaker knew this, the Babtist preacher knew this, everbody in the family knew this. It was just that, when the time came to descend into the earth, I knew he'd feel a little better knowing he got a couple hundred bucks knocked off the price somewhere down the line. I've seen him dramatically walk out of car dealerships while haggling over the last twenty-dollar license fee. So it was a matter of principle. As you live, so should you die.

In the funeral home sales room, Mama and I got the prime seats, the plush armchairs right next to the mahogany table with the casket brochure. The first page of it tells you about the $1,300 you've already spent just having your Dad brought over from the hospital, preserved for a couple days, and embalmed so that Grandma won't go completely to pieces when she sees him. The next figure you see is . . . $14,000.

This is for the solid-bronze casket that lasts longer than King Tut's funerary chapel and includes a CD player and a hot tub. It's the same principle as buying *Encyclopaedia Britannica*. First they show you the $5,000 leather-bound "golden heritage" edition, so when you end up buying the $1,200 cheapskate edition, you feel like you got a great bargain. In my case, it just made me wanna take a look at the $14,000 bronze casket. This was easy enough. The undertaker herded all eight or nine of us into the Casket Showroom, where I went over all the sticker prices to see how much this guy was adding on top of factory invoice. Of course, he was already showing Mama the style we bought last year to bury Grandpa in, so we all knew we weren't gonna beat $2,000. Who's gonna tell Mama that Grandpa's casket had metallic-silver pallbearer handles but Dad doesn't need em? So the only question was, would we trade up or not?

Suddenly Mama whispered in my direction, "You know, none of this is really very important to me."

Bingo! What luck! We're ready to bargain!

Just as suddenly, I lost my advantage. She said, "I like the blue better than the silver, though."

"Okay, Mom," I told her, "you pick out the color." She picked out a navy-blue exterior, light blue upholstery, and we took the same $2,000 middle-class model that Grandpa had.

Next item: the vault. The thing they stick in the ground that goes *around* the casket. I told the guy I never have understood exactly why they use those things, and he told me you had to have one according to state health law. And then he went on about how the steel-reinforced ones would last a whole lot longer than the concrete ones, and the concrete ones would last a whole lot longer than the nonconcrete ones, "but sooner or later, no matter how good your container and your drainage is, any grave is going to eventually cave in."

Cave in! Here's the key word! Something's gonna "cave in" on Daddy! Meanwhile, we're staring at these humongous elephant crates that look like they could survive the sinking of the *Titanic,* and I can see Mama starting to lose it. She's about to point to the one that "we used for Grandpa," and so I kind of motion her into the next room.

"Mom, you know the part of the funeral service where they say 'ashes to ashes, dust to dust'?"

"Yes."

"Well, that means it's *supposed* to cave in. He's *supposed* to become dust. It's the Christian way."

"Oh, well, that makes sense. That's fine with me."

And so we told the guy we'd take the $330 model, least allowable under the rules of a "perpetual care cemetery." And at that moment, I reminded Dad that we had already saved maybe $1,500 in emotional frills. He hated paying for frills so much that, if a product looked too pretty, he mistrusted the price, thinking he might be paying for paint or the package.

Next thing, we headed out to the graveyard. Way out on the county line, where you can save an extra thou or two, next to a couple liquor stores and a nightclub. It took about a half hour for the caretaker to drive us around among the various dead-person subdivisions, with little markers on them reading ETERNAL REST PASTURES and PINES OF PEACE. And all this time he's explaining how we've got to choose between a mausoleum, a flat-marker grave, an upright-marker grave, an *underground* mausoleum (same as a mausoleum, but you wouldn't wanna visit), a roadside plot, a single plot, a double plot, or a family plot.

The sisters and I started talking about the implications of a "family plot." But Mama cut through most of this confusion when she said, "Well, I doubt if anybody else in the family would want to be buried here." She looked at me, but I was so distracted that I started wondering, "Well, you know, maybe I *could* get a deal here."

"No," I told her. "Just you and Dad."

Just saved some more money, I told Dad.

Then the caretaker showed us a few plots, the main price difference being whether they were by the road or not. The ones by the road cost more.

"Do you kids want me and your father to be by the road?"

This is something that none of us kids had considered until that moment, but suddenly it became very important.

"No, Mom," I finally decided. "I think it would be more meaningful if we had to get out of the car first."

"Okay," she said, as if wanting the whole process to come to an end, "how about this area right here?"

The caretaker started flipping through his computer printouts, to make sure there weren't any dead people already sunk into that particular turf.

"This would be available as long as you want a flat marker," he said, and then explained how it's easier to mow the grass if the flat marker is flush with the ground.

"Do you care if the marker is flat or upright?" I asked Mom.

"I'm going to be *under* the marker," she said. "You kids should decide."

So I asked my sisters. Big mistake. To my sisters, a flat marker doesn't "look right." A grave is supposed to have a marker that stands straight up.

"Fine," I told em. We asked the caretaker where the nearest upright-marker place was, and he started fumbling through the computer printouts again.

We finally found a couple of spots right under a big pine tree. Only about ten yards from the road, so that Grandma's wheelchair could make it for the graveside service. Eleven hunnerd bucks each, plus $250 for "opening" the grave.

Toting it all up as we drove back home, I told Mama, "About sixty-five hundred."

"Good," she said.

"Good," my dad said.

He can rest now.

To discuss the meaning of life with Joe Bob, or to get his *We Are the Weird* newsletter, which he bills as "the last uncensored publication in America," write Joe Bob Briggs, P.O. Box 2002, Dallas, TX 75221.

About the Author

JOE BOB BRIGGS is a comedian, syndicated columnist, and TV and radio personality who crawled out from under a large rock somewhere in Texas around 1982. His first newspaper column, "Joe Bob Goes to the Drive-In," championed the lost cause of the American drive-in and its basic elements: "Blood, breasts and beasts." The column was immediately popular and immediately controversial for its free-form lampoons of everything sacred in American life. The Joe Bob philosophy of life ("Life's a fern bar, let's get outta here") eventually led to a second syndicated column, "Joe Bob's America," a three-times-weekly radio show, and a series of sold-out concerts in American cities alive with Joe Bob fever. And, beginning in 1986, Joe Bob started appearing on cable TV's The Movie Channel with his Saturday night program, *Joe Bob's Drive-In Theater.*

Joe Bob's previous books are *Joe Bob Goes to the Drive-In; A Guide to Western Civilization or My Story;* and *Joe Bob Goes Back to the Drive-In.*